13 DEADLY MISTAKES BUSINESSES MAKE WHILE HIRING A DIGITAL AGENCY

GROW YOUR BUSINESS BY 10X

BlueRose ONE.com
Stories Matter
NewDelhi • London

For permission requests, email to the publisher,
Subject "Attention: Permissions Coordinator,"
at the address below.
pc@yourBookWebsite.com

Publisher Name:

Ordering Information:
Quantity sales. Special discounts are available on quantity purchases by corporations, associations, and others. For details, contact the publisher at the address above.

For Ordering outside Dubai, please contact Al Nasr Distribution
: Tel: (+97150) 99999-88888
Visit www.yourBookWebsite.com/international.

References for graphs-Search Engine Journal, Social Media Today, Demographics-Wikipedia

Printed in Dubai
First Edition
14 13 12 11 10 / 10 9 8 7 6 5 4 3 2 1

DEDICATIONS

To my **Husband Kishore**
and my Inspiration my **daughter Anisha**
Without their patience, understanding, support and most above all love,
the completion of this work would not have been possible.

ACKNOWLEDGEMENT

Writing a book is harder than I thought and more rewarding than I could have ever imagined. None of this would have been possible without my family support.

I would like to express my gratitude to the many people who saw me through this book; to all those who provided support, talked things over, read, wrote, offered comments, allowed me to quote their remarks and assisted in the editing, proofreading and design.

Nobody has been more important to me in the pursuit of this project than the members of my family. I would like to thank first my mother Rajni, whose love and guidance is with me in whatever I pursue. Mom, she is my ultimate role model. She taught me discipline, tough love, manners, respect, and so much more that has helped me succeed in life. I truly have no idea where I'd be if she hadn't given me a roof over my head or became the father figure, whom I desperately needed at that early age.

Most importantly, I wish to thank my loving and supportive husband Kishore, and my wonderful amazing daughter and my love, Anisha, who provide unending inspiration. Without whom this book would have not come to life. A family, who has never failed to amaze me, every day.

My darling my brother Ajay, his wife Pooja and their two princesses Akiela and Nikita.

I'm eternally grateful to my team at Digital Sapiens, who took in extra time to manage work, when they didn't have to.

To my Boss Mr. Robert Nicholas, at Nicholas Publishing. He never saw my race, or my lack of experience or the fact that I just delivered. He just saw a human being hungry to learn, hungry to grow, and hungry to succeed in business. He never stopped me, he only encouraged me throughout my working career.

Although this entrepreneurship period of my life was filled with many ups and then downs, my time in the Digital industry was worth it. My time in this industry wouldn't have been made possible without Ajay who taught me the honest Digital game.

A very special thanks to my coaches and all the people who were tough as rock that made me rise through the ups and downs to become the CEO of the company in real terms.

Last but not the least: I beg forgiveness of all those who have been with me over the course of the years and whose names I have failed to mention.

Writing a book about the story of your life is a surreal process, a keen insight, and ongoing support in bringing my stories to life. It is because of all your efforts and encouragement that I have a legacy to pass on to my family, where one didn't exist before.

To everyone at the Digital Sapiens, who enabled me to be the CEO of a company that I'm honored to be a part of. Thank you for letting me serve, for being a part of our amazing company, and for showing up every day and helping more authors turn their ideas into stories.

CONTENTS

13 Mistakes Brands Make
When Hiring Digital Marketing Agencies

Imagine this: A brand comes to an agency looking to turbo charge their digital marketing performance efforts and crush sky-high revenue goals in the process, only to leave the engagement a few months later feeling frustrated and misunderstood. Sound familiar?

It's a scenario that plays out every day in the digital marketing space, and is one even the highest-rated agencies experience. But more often than not, it is caused by a few fundamental mistakes that brands make when hiring and working with a digital marketing agency. Working with hundred plus clients over the past ten years, as the Digital experts, an agency with experience in both international and local market have seen a fair few of these mistakes play out - and learned the best ways brands can combat them. Here, we break down 13 of the most common mistakes brands make when working with digital marketing agencies - from budget woes and miscommunication to ignoring the digital landscape and more - and how to avoid them to ensure your next engagement is a smashing success.

1.Not Choosing a Full Service Agency

Not all agencies are created equal. Some agencies focus on social media marketing, but not so much on creating impactful websites and SEO services. It's vital to realize that these services work best in conjunction as a unit, so you should always go with a digital marketing agency that does it all, from crafting robust websites to generating compelling SEO-based content to Social media marketing and conversions. Is your business looking to save time and stress on deploying an effective marketing strategy?

Then it is crucial to explore a marketing agency that can help you achieve this. A boutique agency and a full-service agency are the two main types of companies that provide various types of attention and expertise.Here we define each type and examine the benefits and differences of each.

While a boutique agency will provide a much more personalized approach to your business's marketing needs, a full-service agency might be able to minimize your budget spend. We give you the full rundown on each, but you need to define your needs, values, and budget before deciding on one or the other. This data shows us that most companies are hiring multiple marketing agencies, likely specialized in various different verticals.

2.What is a boutique agency?

A boutique agency is a smaller advertising agency that provides more customized services and focuses on the client's industry and niche. Boutique agencies center their work on higher-quality branding and strategic and creative projects. Because they are more familiar with a specific niche and/or marketing vertical, they can focus their resources on much more specific marketing initiatives for their clients.

These types of marketing firms do not have multiple locations around the world. They do not have large payrolls, high overhead costs, or have experience working with big brands like Coca-Cola, Nike, or Toyota. But they usually work with smaller and sometimes more demanding big businesses to start ups with hi-pressure on performance EVERYDAY for both business-to-business (B2B) or direct-to-consumer (D2C) companies because they can relate to them.

Although this is typically the case, larger companies can undoubtedly benefit from boutique agencies. Boutique agencies are much more focused on the client's daily needs, and their customer service process is designed to service their current customers to the best of their abilities. These small agencies focus less on salespeople and closing deals but on maintaining existing client relationships.

Still, they direct their attention to their existing team of experts who are always innovating newer, more creative ways of getting things done.

Why You Should Use a Boutique Agency?

There are a variety of reasons why your business could utilize the services of a boutique agency.

Although boutique agencies are more commonly paired with smaller firms, it is becoming much more common for larger companies to seek a boutique agency because of their creative power. Here are some of the primary reasons why a boutique agency could be the answer for you:

a) Relationship and Personal Attention

When you elect to work with a boutique agency, your experience will be much more personable overall. And turn around time for small to big details from competitive analysis to data mining in hours or couple of days just to ensure the client is successful and happy every step of the way.

You will be in direct contact with the knowledge experts and specialists who are dedicated to your brand. You will have direct oversight and interactions with people who are working on the marketing campaigns, but you will also have direct access to the owner or CEO of the company. A lot of people have fancy to deal with the power house of the agency, but it's just a day-in, day-out, ongoing, never-ending, persevering, compassionate kind of activity which makes a boutique agency a powerful fuel for your business engine.

Another key advantage of your relationship with a boutique agency is the overall flow of information and communication between you and the boutique agency's small team. Questions will get delegated much more efficiently, and your answers will get addressed much more quickly. If you see ongoing improvements that need to be made, these can get updated expediently.

b) Flexibility

Because boutique agencies do not provide a one-size-fits-all focus to your business, you can work with them to get a much more personalized, unique marketing plan and you are an important customer to them, not just a mere number, out of their 100 clients.

Boutique agencies have the resources and methodologies to learn about the environment of your businesses inside and out. They will be much more in tune with your challenges, which will enable them to deliver a much more effective strategy.

A boutique agency's flexibility allows them to adapt to your changing needs and requirements continually. Because the boutique agency's company is typically smaller, it will not need to navigate company policies to serve you. They can make meaningful decisions on the fly and offer you dynamic solutions throughout their relationship with you.

c) Innovative Ideas

More extensive, full-service firms will usually deploy the same strategies and methods with each of their clients. They rely on time, and if they see one marketing test work well, they will use it for every customer they take on. On the other hand, boutique agencies do not take advantage of time trials. They can easily adjust and build a customized strategy because their goal is to make your reputation.

Because there is no set way to do things in a boutique marketing plan, the specialists can brainstorm new ideas for each client. Instead of referring to outdated processes and initiatives, boutique agencies will bring a fresh perspective and explore new ways to build your brand presence.

d) Growth

Boutique agencies love helping medium to large sized businesses because their experience makes them a rocket in a lot of ways to turbo charge your business. For the companies which are trying to grow and expense, so working together will be a motivating factor for each party. Each business will have overlapping goals, which allows your relationship to be built upon commonality. Communication flow will be efficient because both companies are genuinely invested in each other.

A boutique agency will usually monitor its growth based on the successes and outcomes of their clients. These agencies are not in it only for the money, but they are working with you because meaningful relationships are vital to sustainable business growth.

For SEO the boutique agencies will use the paid bloggers or their own networks to get you desired results. They thrive that they provide sometimes for additional thought process or give additional value to their clients.

Less Likely To Outsource unlike the Large full service agencies in Dubai, UAE and in the World.

According to a recent survey:

- 68% of full-service large agencies outsource SEO to a white label SEO providers.
- 48% of full-service agencies outsource PPC services
- 28% of full-service agencies outsource content marketing services.

WHAT SERVICES DID YOU OUTSOURCE?
(2021,2022 & 2023)

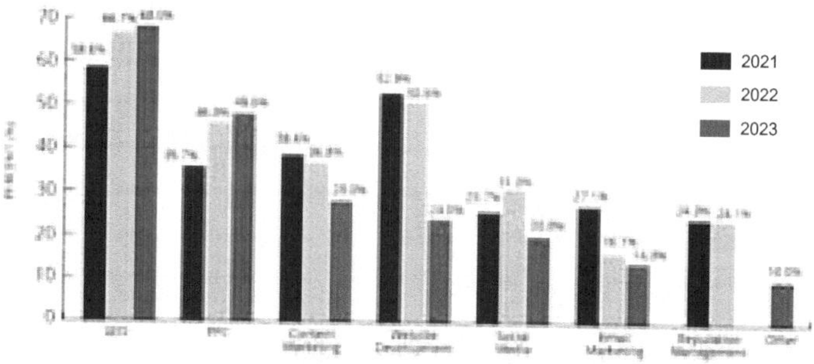

www.semrush.com

It's an open industry secret that full-service agencies will outsource some or almost all of the services.

Many full-service Big to large agencies will focus on a few single areas of marketing expertise and then trust white-label partners like a boutique agency(like us) to handle the rest. If you go with a full-service agency there is really no guarantee that the agency you hired will be doing the complete work for you. To the contrary, it's highly likely that they will not be providing all of your services.

Sometimes clients will check the websites of full-service agencies and read glowing bios of their employees, and think "wow, their staff really knows what they are doing!"

Unfortunately, those people might not be the ones who are handling the project, making the website a little deceitful. Boutique agencies do not outsource because they don't have to. They have all of the specialists that they need right there in their organization.

When you work with a boutique agency you know exactly what you're getting and who you're getting to work on your project. You'll also be able to reach them directly with questions.

1.What is a Full-Service Agency?

A full-service agency is a fully integrated marketing and advertising agency that provides a complete set of services. These larger agencies are designed to handle all advertising and marketing requirements that you and your company might be deployed in-house. And they mainly work with big brands with bigger budgets. They handle the communication with the client and have a strong creative teams.

These activities could include production, SEO, strategic planning, social media, digital marketing, interactive marketing services, and more.

Businesses will usually approach a full-service agency when they discover that their time spent on advertising and marketing diverts attention away from core business activities.

Time is interchangeable with money, so a full-service agency could allow you to get the most out of marketing. And to keep their cost and hassle low, outsource most of the daily work it to different markets or boutique agencies due to low cost and higher margins.

Why You Should Use a Full-Service Agency

There are a few reasons why your business may want to pursue a full service agency. Here are some of the top benefits of having a full service agency take on your marketing initiatives.

Innovation and creativity is there forte:
Marketing services will not be a low expense for you, but you can get the most bang for your buck with a full service agency. While it might seem questionable to spend the money on a marketing team upfront, it can save you in the long run. If you hire agencies or individuals who specialize in a narrow niche or industry, they can cost you a lot more.

Saves Time

No matter how large or small your team or business is, you will need to utilize some marketing strategy to grow. It usually takes a team, and your current staff may have its hands in multiple buckets. If you elect to use a full-service agency, you have a group of people who can focus 100% of their knowledge on developing your marketing.

Diversity and Flexibility

A full service agency is built to get your project done correctly and under budget. Regardless of what your request might be, a full-service agency will have someone that can do it. Although responsiveness might not be as quick as a boutique agency, you can rest assured that a full-service agency has the resources to address and fulfill your request.

2. Which is the better option: Boutique or Full-Service Agency?

You and your business need to define your budget, values, current needs, and growth potential before deciding on the right type of agency. Both options can provide valuable marketing solutions for your business. However, Boutique agency is team of people working on selective businesses and getting kick from their success. And a larger agency has many client relationship managers and handle various projects/accounts along with yours. Normally, if you have an international tie up with the big agency from your headquarters in Europe or America then your choice is limited and this does benefit the larger agencies to keep big clients to themselves with not really looking at real benefit for the client in local markets. Which is the a great old way of working for off-line mediums. However, in 2023 it is local, location based on a user's location, geo-targeted marketing sends personalized messages. If a consumer has opted in to let an app access their location, they may get messages in the app or push notifications based on region or proximity to a store. Geotargeting works based on IP addresses. Every connected device has a unique IP address making them identifiable. From there, device IP addresses can be matched to country, postal code, etc. to determine where users are located.

Geofencing:

Geofence marketing is proven to increase sales, engagement, and customer loyalty. Geofencing marketing is specific location-based advertisements that allow marketing teams to target their advertising and content delivery based on the targeted area. A "geofence" is the physical boundaries of a target location. It could be a specific city, a postal code, a county, or a kilometer range around a physical store location. It is also possible to configure multiple geofenced marketing channels for businesses with multiple locations. With geofencing marketing, marketers can resonate more strongly with the people living in those locations.

Also your understanding of the psychometric of the local population-where they eat, how they eat, drink, buy, love, share, explore, learn and behave offline is aligned to online behaviours.

If you are focused on quality and personal attention, then the boutique agency is your ideal option.

Boutique agencies will take the extra time and focus on learning your situation and world, designing a marketing plan customized for your company, and then execute it and provide education on ongoing improvements.

These agencies are also much more responsive and attentive to your continually changing needs.

But if you are operating on a lower budget and do not have the time to talk through marketing ideas throughout the week continually, you could elect to go with the full-service agency.

You can tell them what you need to get done, and then they will deploy it for you. These day with chat GPT 4 AI version you can automate a lot of your work. You may not get the most personalized marketing solutions through them, but you will most likely save time and get some results.

Now that you know the benefits of each agency type, would we be good marketers if we didn't tell you to take a deeper look into Digital Media in Dubai. Browse around and get in touch so you can take the next step in building your brand presence!

3. Not Having a Clear Understanding of Your Marketing Budget

You don't need to know exactly how much money you should be spending on digital marketing, but you should have a good idea of how much you're willing to spend as well as the full scope of cost to take on certain marketing efforts before you engage with an agency. Once you have that ballpark budget, you should then work with your agency's experts to understand where that money should actually be spent to maximize its value and ask for estimations for results/leads/visibility as per your goal. You may come in thinking you only need to focus on search engine marketing, but listen when the experts tell you that investing in your owned and operated blog or revamping your website are critical uses for your marketing budget.

Remember: there are two sides to the budget coin when it comes to working with agencies. So having a good understanding of how much money you'll save in the long run by outsourcing your digital marketing efforts instead of doing it in-house (and how that in-house talent can be best used instead and will be rusty after some time as working on same vertical) will help put your budget into perspective. And as we all know, CHANGE is the other name of Digital Marketing.

Easy is look at your 5 year goal and your 10 year goal then work backwards to your conversion ratio of each lead to meeting to sale ratio. When you have these numbers you know what is the number of leads you need per month. Ask your boutique agency to give you estimated leads before you sign up with them. And all you have ensure that the leads you are getting in one month are aligned with your 10 year goal. Simple isnt it?

Source: Getty images

Not Tracking Results. It is possible to determine which campaign is bringing in the most leads, and which of those leads convert. You will have to work hard to get the last bit of conversion information out of your CRM (or your salespeople), but it is possible. And once you have that information, you can make better decisions about which channels, methods, and messages are doing you the most good.

Misaligning Incentives With Your Agency

One of the best ways to ensure your budget is maximized is to take a look at the pricing model of your agency. Revenue share models can make agencies short-sighted and far more likely to employ quick-fix money making solutions that will actually tarnish your brand in the long run. On the flip side, paying your agency by the hour can make them work slowly. Instead, look for agencies that operate on a per-project basis or employ management fees without any long-term contracts (like here at Digital Sapiens) — that way, the incentives to boost your brand in the right way are evenly spread.

Source: Getty images

The rate of change in the media landscape over the past 20+ years has been unprecedented, and this is not new news to marketers. The internet and innovative work in the digital technology space have been platforms for change that have allowed for new ideas to sprout and take reign, with some of those ideas surpassing traditional media channels both in use and performance over time. Digital has enabled brands to move on from a solely 'broadcast' philosophy (e.g., OOH, TVC) to one that also encompasses the ability for a more integrated, targeted marketing approach (e.g., programmatic, affiliate, social media, retargeting the funnel). This is not to say, however, that marketing activity aimed at achieving broad reach doesn't still have its place at the top of the hierarchy of a marketer's needs but what is important is to understand how the media landscape is changing and what a business must do to be ready to win in this space, both now and for the future.

01 - Crossing new bridges

An example of how this transformation has manifested can be seen in the most traditional of media formats which have only ever been thought of as tools to drive awareness. Brands can include calls-to-action that are digitally led in their television commercials (e.g., download an app, visit a website, or subscription) or even develop digital strategies that compliment traditional methods (e.g., increasing SEM spend during a TV campaign). Digital out-of-home posters allow for the adaptation of messaging in real-time to build relevancy (e.g., a beer brand featuring the weather temperature in its messaging on a hot day) or feature calls-to-action that make that asset work harder by driving dwell time on user devices via tools like QR codes.

Digital has built a bridge between the conversion driving functions and awareness driving functions of businesses – the problem that needs addressing is the lack of marketers utilising the bridge in their plans.

02 - Aligning motivations

A mistake I've seen many a brand business make is the level of responsibility they give to agencies in steering the strategy conversation – I've sat in rooms where one could have easily mistaken the agency strategy director as the gatekeeper of the brand while the brand lead being quietly present in the same room (this is far too common). Now, before I make the mistake of having this perceived as an agency bashing, I'd like to add a disclaimer – there are many great agencies that do fantastic work for their clients. I'd like to think that most do! The trends I'm addressing tend to be found in larger organisations where the volume of work is higher, the clients are larger in both size and revenue and therefore driving efficiencies by 'grouping' supplier deals and offering 'added value' becomes much more feasible and common in practice. It is this model that I am concerned with. Agencies are founded on an incentive model that doesn't always work out best for the brand - in fact, it is guaranteed not to. Agencies profit through acquiring as many clients as they can while also reaping the benefits of the deals they get in place with media companies that client investment will inevitably trickle down to. The more the client spends, the more the agency benefits. This is not to say that agencies shouldn't make money – it's about the method they use to generate said revenue and the motivations that these methods are founded on.

For example, a brand is incentivised to drive business performance, which includes driving costs down while driving profitability up wherever necessary and/or possible. An agency is both incentivised to support the client in delivering on their objectives with the best solutions and expertise, while also having underlying incentives with media companies (which tend to be founded on volume, not value) that may sway the type of consultation the client receives as a result. This misalignment of incentives makes for an untrustworthy love triangle that you certainly won't see me taking my trousers off for in risk of being mugged.

03 - Short termism = death

The change we have seen occur in the media landscape over the past 10+ years has also blind-sided many marketers. There is a tendency to get excited by just how 'real-time' one can get insofar as extracting insights from data and developing an action plan as a result. This tendency by marketers has morphed into an appetite to sought for strategies that deliver short-term results. However, thanks to the work of Agency teams, we're reminded that marketers should never take their eyes off the long-term ball since this is the game that will deliver healthy brand metrics and with that longevity in existence. Short spikes in an upward trajectory have immediate steep drops, whereas long-term brand building activity provide the foundation for scalability.

04 - Playing hide and seek

To drive some form of organisational change within a business, an area that needs to be addressed in parallel is that of business culture. A culture that rejects change will not experience the most seamless of transitions – instead, it will encounter friction. This is where language becomes key and terms such as ‘innovation’ and ‘test and learn’ make the idea of change more accessible since these words allude to a feeling of exploration rather than one of forced adaptation. Such terminology has contributed positively to the adoption of adaptation, especially amongst those who fear change.

However, the risk we ride today is that these terms are now being used to bucket and silo thinking and functions in ways that are detrimental to a business. The word ‘digital’ belongs not to a specific group of specialists but to everybody – everybody bears a responsibility to understand how digital can play a role in better enabling them in their responsibilities. Where it was once a specific business function’s responsibility to bring a business into the digital era through a ‘transformation period’ (key word being ‘period’ that has a start and end date) it is now a shared responsibility. The rate of change in the digital landscape is constant, therefore the necessity to adopt digital in one’s sphere of responsibilities is critical – unless, of course, you’d rather hide behind the term ‘transformation’ as an endless state for which others are responsible on your behalf… I can guarantee that you will fall behind if you pursue the latter. It’s one thing to evolve a businesses infrastructure through digital transformation, however if ‘digital’ is not considered a shared responsibility culturally, the aftermath of the transformation will be one of stagnation.

The risk of living in a world where digital is only ever tied to terms such as 'innovation' and 'test and learn' is being left behind by competitors as a result since, let's face it, the innovation budget is the first to get cut when the going gets tough.

05 - Fragmentation and decentralisation

One theme with a growing audience of interest insofar as how it can transform society is that of decentralisation. Technology is driving fragmentation of marketplaces on many fronts and a method to deal with fragmentation is to decentralise the powers that participate. Currently, most businesses are set up as organisations that centralise power management and distribute responsibilities and actions from a core that consists of what they believe to be the leading experts and best decision-makers. To fully harness the power of digital in media, localisation is key. Local talent that understands local technology (i.e., marketplace fragmentation) and local culture is important to maximise the opportunity. Being in an open-planned office doesn't 'do the trick'.

The 5 themes I've touched on highlight some of the barriers that I believe can cause a business to stagnate and as a result fall behind competitors. Those that are falling behind are, likely without knowing it, creating their own barriers and are masters of the own demise. Does this apply to you and your 'patch' of responsibilities (I use the word 'patch' in jest)? Are you contented that your partners are as motivated as you and are marching towards the same objectives? Is your business bucketing and siloing responsibilities that could be broadened in adoption and responsibility?

4. Assuming That Digital Marketing Is Only About Transactions

When it comes to maximizing your marketing budget, it also pays to remember that returns aren't the only measure of marketing success. If you're only allowing your digital marketing efforts to drive direct response and forgoing brand-building strategies, you could be setting yourself up to struggle in the long term. So don't pigeonhole your agency to typical acquisition channels and instead embrace a full-funnel approach that supports multiple, necessary touchpoints for the customer journey. You'll create an audience that is more likely to be engaged for the long-haul if you do.

Source: Getty images

The development of digital marketing has immensely altered the marketing scene. It has given all organisations a chance to market and advertise their brand on a global platform, majorly growing their possible target audience.

This further digitisation of the marketing scene has also had an effect on how consumers interact and associate with the different available organisations and brands.

How digital marketing influences consumer behavior:

Consumers never make a purchase prior to conducting online research Consumers now have the ability to collect all the research they could possibly need, as well as compare brands before making an informed decision followed by a fitting purchase.

The consumer's decision regarding which product to purchase is heavily impacted by all the information they find while researching about the product. This makes it absolutely crucial for brands and businesses to have a strong online presence, as this is what consumers judge them on. A brand's online presence can communicate its message more clearly and accurately considering it's the business who controls the information placed online.

This impacts consumer behaviour since today, brand presence is a combination of associations, such as values, products and ideals, made by consumers after they have interacted with your business. An online presence is also a means to communicate directly with costumers, this translates to a one-on-one communication medium with both happy and dissatisfied customers.

Nowadays, we can see a very steep decline in print advertising. It is estimated that the print advertising revenue from newspapers will decrease to 5.3 billion dollars by 2024 in comparison to the estimated 25.20 billion dollar revenue it procured in 2017.

This makes an online presence crucial as it is the first point of communication between a brand a customer, a brand's response to both praise and criticism is done through digital platforms, making a brand's digital presence crucial to its survival.

The powerful tool of digital word-of-mouth

A dependable way to get recommendations is through digital word-of-mouth, also called influencer marketing. Digital word-of-mouth, also known as influencer marketing is a dependable method of recommendation.

Consumers today seek recommendations from peers or look for endorsements from their role models. In addition to customer reviews, influencer marketing, testimonials, and comments, other types of recommendations can also assist brands in establishing trust with consumers. Customers are more likely to trust a brand if it has a good digital word of mouth.

Businesses have also been able to maintain a presence online through this. Word-of-mouth can have a huge impact on any brand's sales. Furthermore, it is safe to assume that digital marketing has placed consumers in control.

Unreliable clientele loyalty

Prior to the digitisation of the marketing world, customers were more prone to staying partial to their brand of choice. They chose to stick to the brand they are already familiar with, this was a result of low exposure to the different available products on the market. Today, customers actively search for different products that cost the same but provide them with increased value.

Customers now feel less hesitation when replacing their go-to brands with brand new ones, this is because customers are now able to judge a product based on a range of different criteria including sales and discounts, value, and customer support. Since customers are able to research everything they need to know, if they find a better deal they are more likely to take it.

There are three pricing models for digital agencies—hourly, milestones, and value-based.

- Hourly is about charging for the inputs - the hours your team puts into the work.
- Milestone is about charging for the outputs - your team's deliverables.
- Value - Based is about charging for the results - the business impact of your work.

The last one is beneficial for the client and the Agency. However, in Dubai normally, agencies and clients prefer the milestone model mainly.

Consumers exhibit a lower level of patience

Nowadays, consumers demand fast responses to their questions and concerns. Digital marketing makes this possible. You can easily share customer queries and thoughts on social media for a large audience. Positive and negative customer reviews greatly influence consumers.

By empowering customers and giving them tailored experiences, digital marketing allows brands to establish transparent and stronger relationships with them. Consequently, digital marketing is a strong motivator for consumers.

Impulse buying is driven by digital marketing

Marketing through digital media allows brands to promote their products at the right time and in the right place where consumers are most likely to make spontaneous or impulsive purchases. Deals, discounts, and offers from brands are used to entice customers to buy their products. It's highly unlikely to happen in an offline setting, but it can be used by marketers as a marketing tactic. Provides consumers with a more customized shopping experience

Digital marketing allows consumers to tailor their shopping experiences. It has been observed that customers prefer instant gratification to researching new products. A brand's digital content can be crafted and modified to offer tailored shopping experiences. This will have a significant impact on consumer purchases.

4. Skipping the Foundational Work

In a rush to spend money on ads or redesign their website, many companies forget how integral branding is to driving customer awareness and trust. So allow your agency to take the time to assess your product-market fit, audit your website conversions and analyze your competitive landscape and foundational brand messaging (unique selling propositions, key differentiators, brand pyramid, etc.). Then, set baseline KPIs and marketing goals. Having this strong understanding with your agency will set your big campaigns and launches up for maximum success.

With how accessible the internet is today, would you believe me if I told you the number of people who go online every day is still increasing?

Source: Getty images

It is. In fact, there are about 4.9 billion global internet users as of 2021, a 400 million jump from 2020(in one year). And although we say it a lot, the way people shop and buy really has changed along with it — meaning offline marketing can't be your only strategy for driving sales because you need to meet audiences where they're already spending time: on the internet.

Marketing has always been about connecting with your audience in the right place and at the right time. Today, that means you need to meet them where they are already spending time: on the internet.

Digital marketing — in other words, any form of online marketing.

At our boutique agency, we talk a lot about inbound marketing as a really effective way to attract, engage, and delight customers online. But we still get a lot of questions from people all around the world about digital marketing. Keep reading to see how digital marketing is carried out today.

What is digital marketing?

Why is digital marketing important?

Types of Digital Marketing

What does a digital marketer do?

Inbound Marketing vs. Digital Marketing: Which is it?

Does digital marketing work for all businesses?

How to Do Digital Marketing

Digital Marketing Examples

So, how do you define digital marketing today?

5.What is digital marketing?

Digital marketing, also called online marketing, refers to all marketing efforts that occur on the internet. Businesses leverage digital channels such as search engines, social media, email, and other websites to connect with current and prospective customers. This also includes communication through text or multimedia messages.

A seasoned inbound marketer might say inbound marketing and digital marketing are virtually the same thing, but there are some minor differences. And conversations with marketers and business owners in the UAE, U.S., U.K., Asia, Australia, and New Zealand, I've learned a lot about how those small differences are being observed across the world.

How does a business define digital marketing?

At this stage, digital marketing is vital for your business and brand awareness. It seems like every other brand has a website, and if they don't, they at least have a social media presence or digital ad strategy. Digital content and marketing is so common that consumers now expect and rely on it as a way to learn about brands. Because digital marketing has so many possibilities, you can get creative and experiment with a variety of marketing tactics on a budget. And the communication strategy is vital -what communication, at what time and what stage of brand development is the core of business growth.

Overall, digital marketing with creative videos, communication leaving an impact on our customers mind through all social, digital, GDN, programmatic channel is the key looping in all the news papers with high trust from the customer will bring in trust to your brand aligning with influencer marketing is defined by using numerous digital tactics and channels to connect with customers where they spend much of their time: online. The best digital marketers have a clear picture of how each digital marketing campaign supports their overarching goals. And depending on the goals of their marketing strategy, marketers can support a larger campaign through the free and paid channels at their disposal.

A content marketer, for example, could create a series of blog posts that generate leads from an ebook. A social media marketer might help promote those blogs through paid and organic posts on the business's social media accounts, and the email marketer could create an email campaign to send those who download the ebook more information on the company.

We'll talk more about these specific digital marketers as we go along.

Digital marketing helps you reach a larger audience than you could through traditional methods and target the prospects who are most likely to buy your product or service. Digital Marketing gives you numbers and in business the only TRUTH IS NUMBERS IN A BUSINESS and everything else is a story. Additionally, it's often more cost-effective than traditional advertising and enables you to measure success on a daily basis and pivot as you see fit.

There are a few major benefits of digital marketing:

» You can focus your efforts on only the prospects most likely to purchase your product or service.

» It's more cost-effective than outbound marketing methods.

» Digital marketing evens the playing field within your industry and allows you to compete with bigger brands.

» Digital marketing is measurable with numbers.

» It's easier to adapt and change a digital marketing strategy.

» Digital marketing can improve your conversion rate and the quality of your leads.

» You can engage audiences at every stage with digital marketing.

Let's dive deeper.

1. You can focus your efforts on only the prospects most likely to purchase your product or service.

If you place an advertisement on TV, in a magazine, or on a billboard, you have limited control over who sees the ad. Of course, you can measure certain demographics — including the magazine's typical readership or the demographic of a certain neighborhood — but it's still largely a shot in the dark.

Digital marketing allows you to identify and target a highly-specific audience with personalized and high-converting marketing messages.

For instance, you might use social media targeting to show ads to a certain audience based on variables like age, gender, location, interests, networks, or behaviors. Alternatively, you might use PPC or SEO strategies to serve ads to users who've shown interest in or searched for specific keywords related to your product, service, or industry.

Ultimately, digital marketing helps you conduct the research necessary to identify your buyer personas and refine your strategy to ensure you're reaching prospects most likely to buy.

2. It's more cost-effective than outbound marketing methods.

Digital marketing helps you track day-to-day campaign performance, so you know what channels are performing well and which aren't, helping you optimize your campaign budgets for high ROI. The same can't be said for traditional forms of advertising. It doesn't matter how your billboard performs — it still costs the same, even if it doesn't convert.

Plus, with digital marketing, you have complete control over where you choose to spend your money and creatives can be changed with a spur of second. Unlike in traditional medium once the ad is published in Gulf News or magazine, it cannot be undone. Perhaps you spend money on design software to create high-converting Instagram content rather than paying for PPC campaigns. A digital marketing strategy allows you to pivot continuously, ensuring you never waste money on channels and mediums that don't perform well.

By and large, digital marketing is a more cost-effective solution and provides unique opportunities to ensure you get the most bang for your buck.

For instance, if you work for a small business with a limited budget, you might try investing in social media, blogging, or SEO – three strategies that can give you high ROI even with minimal spending.

3. Digital marketing evens the playing field within your industry and allows you to compete with bigger brands.

If you work for a small business, it's likely difficult for you to compete with the major brands in your industry, many of which have millions of dollars to invest in campaigns. Fortunately, there are plenty of opportunities to outrank the big players through strategic digital marketing initiatives.

For instance, you might use long-tail keywords to create high-quality content that ranks on search engines. Search engines don't care which brand is the biggest, but it does care about prioritizing content that resonates best with target audiences.

4. Digital marketing is measurable.

While traditional advertising can be helpful for specific goals, its biggest limitation is measurability. This is one of the biggest benefits of digital marketing, as it can give you a start-to-finish view of all the metrics that matter to your company — including impressions, shares, views, clicks, and time on page.

Unlike most offline marketing efforts, digital marketing allows marketers to see accurate results in real-time. If you've ever put an advertisement in a newspaper, you'll know how difficult it is to estimate how many people flipped to that page and paid attention to it. There's no surefire way to know if that ad was responsible for any sales at all.

On the other hand, with digital marketing, you can measure the ROI of pretty much any aspect of your marketing efforts.

Here are some examples:

Website Traffic

With digital marketing, you can see the exact number of people who have viewed your website's homepage in real-time by using digital analytics software available in marketing platforms.

You can also see how many pages they visited, what device they were using, and where they came from, amongst other digital analytics data.

This intelligence helps you prioritize which marketing channels to spend more or less time on based on the number of people those channels drive to your website. For example, if only 10% of your traffic is coming from organic search, you know that you probably need to spend some time on SEO to increase that percentage. With offline marketing, it can be difficult to tell how people interact with your brand before they interact with a salesperson or make a purchase. With digital marketing, you can identify trends and patterns in people's behavior before they've reached the final stage in their buyer's journey, meaning you can make more informed decisions about how to attract them to your website right at the top of the marketing funnel.

Content Performance and Lead Generation

Imagine you've created a product brochure and posted it through people's letterboxes — that brochure is a form of offline content. The problem is that you have no idea how many people opened your brochure or threw it straight into the trash.

Instead, imagine you have that brochure on your website. You can measure exactly how many people viewed the page it's on, and you can use a form to collect the contact information of those who downloaded it. It's twofold: you measure how many people engage with your content and generate qualified leads when people download it.

Attribution Modeling

An effective digital marketing strategy combined with the right tools and technologies allows you to trace all of your sales back to a customer's first digital touchpoint with your business.

We call this attribution modeling, and it allows you to identify trends in the way people research and buy your product, helping you to make more informed decisions about what parts of your marketing strategy deserve more attention, and what parts of your sales cycle need refining.

Connecting the dots between marketing and sales is hugely important. According to LinkedIn, 87% of sales and marketing leaders say collaboration between sales and marketing enables critical business growth, but misalignment between both teams can damage financial performance. If you can improve your customer's journey through the buying cycle by using digital technologies, then it's likely to reflect positively on your business's bottom line.

5. It's easier to adapt and change a digital marketing strategy.

A lot of work goes into developing a marketing strategy. Generally, you will follow through with that strategy until completion, allow it to take effect, and then judge its results.

However, things do not always go according to plan. You may realize halfway through that a calculation was off, an assumption was incorrect, or an audience did not react how they were expected to. Being able to pivot or adjust the strategy along the way is highly beneficial because it prevents you from having to start over completely.

Being able to change your strategy easily is a great benefit of digital marketing. Adapting a digital marketing strategy is a lot easier than other, more traditional forms of marketing, like mailers or billboard advertising. For instance, if an online ad isn't delivering as expected, you can quickly adjust it or pause it to yield better results.

6. Digital marketing can improve your conversion rate and the quality of your leads.

As digital marketing makes it simpler to measure your marketing efforts, this makes improving your conversion rate simpler as well. Being able to measure the effectiveness of each tactic helps you develop better strategies. Continuously refining your methods improves your conversion rate. Investing in online marketing ensures that everything is optimized for the highest amount of conversions.

Additionally, all leads do not offer the same value for your business. Digital marketing allows you to target a specific audience that will yield higher-quality leads that are more likely to become customers. Connecting your business with the most valuable leads will directly improve your conversion rate.

7. You can engage audiences at every stage with digital marketing.

It's essential to begin engaging your audience as early as possible. Making a connection at the first stage of the buyer's journey helps push the lead through the customer funnel. Using digital marketing allows you to accomplish that from start to finish and at every point in between.

Online channels allow you to follow the entire buying journey of your customers. Understanding and analyzing how customers are move and operate is important for converting leads. Digital marketing allows you to track them through that process. And, even if they don't convert in the early stages, it at least helps ensure they have made a connection with your business.

6.Types of Digital Marketing

- Search Engine Optimization (SEO)
- Content Marketing
- Social Media Marketing
- Pay Per Click (PPC)
- Affiliate Marketing
- Native Advertising
- Marketing Automation
- Email Marketing
- Online PR
- Inbound Marketing
- Sponsored Content
- Search Engine Marketing (SEM)
- Instant Messaging Marketing

Here's a quick rundown of some of the most common digital marketing tactics and the channels involved in each one.

1. Search Engine Optimization (SEO)

This is the process of optimizing your website to "rank" higher in search engine results pages, thereby increasing the amount of organic (or free) traffic your website receives. The channels that benefit from SEO include websites, blogs, and infographics.

There are a number of ways to approach SEO in order to generate qualified traffic to your website. These include:

On-page SEO: This type of SEO focuses on all of the content that exists "on the page" when looking at a website. By researching keywords for their search volume and intent (or meaning), you can answer questions for readers and rank higher on the search engine results pages (SERPs) those questions produce.

Off page SEO: This type of SEO focuses on all of the activity that takes place "off the page" when looking to optimize your website. "What activity not on my own website could affect my ranking?" You might ask. The answer is inbound links, also known as backlinks. The number of publishers that link to you, and the relative "authority" of those publishers, affect how highly you rank for the keywords you care about. By networking with other publishers, writing guest posts on these websites (and linking back to your website), and generating external attention, you can earn the backlinks you need to move your website up on all the right SERPs.

Technical SEO:

This type of SEO focuses on the backend of your website, and how your pages are coded. Image compression, structured data, and CSS file optimization are all forms of technical SEO that can increase your website's loading speed — an important ranking factor in the eyes of search engines like Google.

For a real-life example on how to successfully implement SEO into your digital marketing strategy, check out our case study on Canva here:

2. Content Marketing

This term denotes the creation and promotion of content assets for the purpose of generating brand awareness, traffic growth, lead generation, and customers.

Want to learn and apply content marketing to your business? The channels that can play a part in your content marketing strategy include:

Blog posts: Writing and publishing articles on a company blog helps you demonstrate your industry expertise and generates organic search traffic for your business. This ultimately gives you more opportunities to convert website visitors into leads for your sales team.

Ebooks and whitepapers: Ebooks, whitepapers, and similar long-form content helps further educate website visitors. It also allows you to exchange content for a reader's contact information, generating leads for your company and moving people through the buyer's journey.

Infographics: Sometimes, readers want you to show, not tell. Infographics are a form of visual content that helps website visitors visualize a concept you want to help them learn.

Audio or visual content: Television and radio are popular channels for digital marketing. Creating content that can be shared online as a video or heard on the radio by listeners can greatly broaden your potential

3. Social Media Marketing

This practice promotes your brand and your content on social media channels to increase brand awareness, drive traffic, and generate leads for your business.

If you're new to social platforms, you can use many free tools available at google workspace to connect channels like LinkedIn and Facebook in one place. This way, you can easily schedule content for multiple channels at once and monitor analytics from the platform as well.

On top of connecting social accounts for posting purposes, you can also integrate your social media inboxes into social media channels like —-, so you can get your direct messages in one place.

The channels you can use in social media marketing include:

- Facebook
- Twitter
- LinkedIn
- Instagram
- Snapchat
- Pinterest

Many marketers will use these social media platforms to create a viral campaign. Partnering with a popular content creator or taking part in a trend that resonates with a wide audience is a viral marketing strategy. The purpose is to create something shareworthy in the hopes that it will organically spread across a social media channel.

Don't know how to get started with social media marketing? Download our free social media content calendar to get your social strategy up and running.

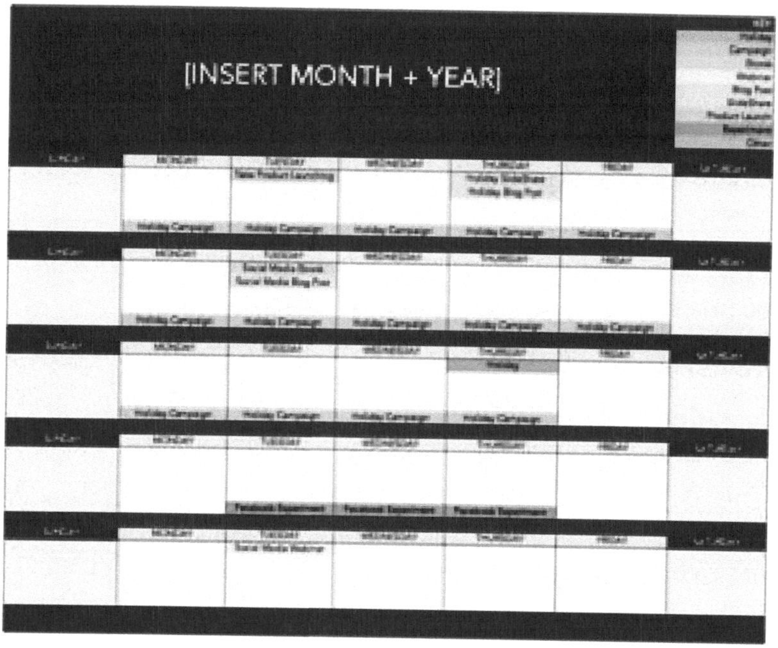

4. Pay Per Click (PPC)

PPC drives traffic to your website by paying a publisher every time your ad is clicked. One of the most common type of PPC is Google Ads, which allows you to pay for top slots on

Google'ssearch engine results pages at a price "per click" of the links you place. Other channels where you can use PPC include:

Paid ads on Facebook: Here, users can pay to customize a video, image post, or slideshow, which Facebook will publish to the news feeds of people who match your business's audience.

Twitter Ads campaigns: Here, users can pay to place a series of posts or profile badges to the news feeds of a specific audience, all dedicated to accomplishing a specific goal for your business. This goal can be website traffic, more Twitter followers, tweet engagement, or even app downloads.

Sponsored Messages on LinkedIn: Here, users can pay to send messages directly to specific LinkedIn users based on their industry and background.

PPC can be hard to grasp at first, so we've created a beginner-friendly guide to get you started.

5. Affiliate Marketing

This is a type of performance-based advertising where you receive a commission for promoting someone else's products or services on your website. Affiliate marketing channels include:

- Hosting video ads through the YouTube Partner Program.
- Posting affiliate links from your social media accounts.

This is part of the relatively new wave of influencer marketing. Creating a campaign using influencers can be a highly effective form of affiliate marketing. Finding the right content creators can take your digital campaign to the next level.

6. Native Advertising

Native advertising refers to advertisements that are primarily content-led and featured on a platform alongside other, non-paid content. BuzzFeed-sponsored posts are a good example, but many people also consider social media advertising to be "native" — Facebook advertising and Instagram advertising, for example.

7. Marketing Automation

Marketing automation refers to the software that automates your basic marketing operations. Many marketing departments can automate repetitive tasks they would otherwise do manually, such as:
Email newsletters: Email automation doesn't just allow you to automatically send emails to your subscribers. It can also help you shrink and expand your contact list as needed so your newsletters are only going to the people who want to see them in their inboxes.

Social media post scheduling: If you want to grow your organization's presence on a social network, you need to post frequently. This makes manual posting a bit of an unruly process. Social media scheduling tools push your content to your social media channels for you, so you can spend more time focusing on content strategy.

Lead-nurturing workflows: Generating leads, and converting those leads into customers, can be a long process.You can automate that process by sending leads specific emails and content once they fit certain criteria, such as when they download and open an ebook.

Campaign tracking and reporting: Marketing campaigns can include a ton of different people, emails, content, webpages, phone calls, and more. Marketing automation can help you sort everything you work on by the campaign it's serving and then track the performance of that campaign based on the progress all of these components make over time.

8. Email Marketing

Companies use email marketing as a way of communicating with their audiences. Email is often used to promote content, discounts and events, as well as to direct people toward the business's website. The types of emails you might send in an email marketing campaign include:

- Blog subscription newsletters.
- Follow-up emails to website visitors who downloaded something.
- Customer welcome emails.
- Holiday promotions to loyalty program members.
- Tips or similar series emails for customer nurturing.

9. Online PR

Online PR is the practice of securing earned online coverage with digital publications, blogs, and other content-based websites. It's much like traditional PR but in the online space. The channels you can use to maximize your PR efforts include:

Reporter outreach via social media: Talking to journalists on Twitter, for example, is a great way to develop a relationship with the press that produces earned media opportunities for your company. Engaging online reviews of your company: When someone reviews your company online, whether that review is good or bad, your instinct might be not to touch it. On the contrary, engaging company reviews helps you humanize your brand and deliver powerful messaging that protects your reputation.

Engaging comments on your personal website or blog: Similar to how you'd respond to reviews of your company, responding to the people reading your content is the best way to generate productive conversation around your industry. If you don't have a dedicated PR team, it can be hard to get started. Luckily, we've got you covered with a boutique approach.

10. Inbound Marketing

Inbound marketing refers to a marketing methodology wherein you attract, engage, and delight customers at every stage of the buyer's journey. You can use every digital marketing tactic listed above throughout an inbound marketing strategy to create a customer experience that works with the customer, not against them. Here are some classic examples of inbound marketing versus traditional marketing:

- Blogging vs. pop-up ads
- Video marketing vs. commercial advertising
- Email contact lists vs. email spam

11. Sponsored Content

With sponsored content, you, as a brand, pay another company or entity to create and promote content that discusses your brand or service in some way. One popular type of sponsored content is influencer marketing. With this type of sponsored content, a brand sponsors an influencer in its industry to publish posts or videos related to the company on social media. Another type of sponsored content could be a blog post or article highlighting a topic, service, or brand.

12. Search Engine Marketing (SEM)

When a potential lead is searching for a product or business related to yours, it's a great opportunity for a promotion. Paid advertising and SEO are two great strategies for promoting your business to capitalize on those future leads. Search engine marketing is another way to increase website traffic by placing paid ads on search engines. The two most popular SEM services are Bing Ads and Google Ads. These paid ads fit seamlessly on the top of search engine results pages, giving instant visibility. This is also an example of effective native advertising.

13. Instant Messaging Marketing

Marketing your products through messaging platforms is a fast way to reach potential leads, even for those who haven't offered up their cell phone number. It's a simple way to let your audience know about flash sales, new products, or updates about their orders. If your customers have questions or need more information, it's also a convenient way for them to connect to customer service. You can send messages directly to a mobile phone via text or on platforms like Facebook Messenger or WhatsApp.

7.What does a digital marketer do?

Digital marketers are in charge of driving brand awareness and lead generation through all the digital channels — both free and paid — that are at a company's disposal. These channels include social media, the company's own website, search engine rankings, email, display advertising, and the company's blog.

The digital marketer focuses on each channel's key performance indicators (KPIs) to properly measure performance. For example, a digital marketer in charge of SEO might measure their website's organic traffic.

At small companies, one person might own many digital channels and tactics described above, while larger companies typically have a specialist focused on one or two brand channels.

Here are some examples of these specialists:

SEO Manager
Main KPIs: Organic traffic

SEO managers work to rank a business on Google SERPs. Using various SEO strategies, this person might work directly with content creators to ensure the content is high-quality and up to Google's standards, even if the company also posts this content on social media.

Content Marketing Specialist

Main KPIs: Time on page, overall blog traffic, YouTube channel subscribers Content marketing specialists are digital content creators. They might keep track of a blogging calendar, or develop a content strategy that includes video. They often work with people in other departments to ensure products and campaigns are supported by promotional content on all digital channels.

Social Media Manager

Main KPIs: Follows, Impressions, Shares A social media manager's role depends on each company and industry. But above all, social media managers manage social media by establishing a posting schedule for the company's written and visual content. They might also work with a content marketing specialist to develop a strategy for which content to share on social media. (Note: Per the KPIs above, "impressions" refers to the number of times a business's posts appear on the newsfeed of a user.)

Marketing Automation Coordinator

Main KPIs: Email open rate, campaign click-through rate, lead-generation (conversion) rate A marketing automation coordinator helps choose and manage the software a marketing team uses to understand customer behavior and measure business growth. Many of the marketing operations described above might be executed separately, so it's important for there to be someone who can group these activities into individual campaigns and track performance.

Inbound Marketing vs. Digital Marketing: Which Is It?

Inbound marketing is a methodology that uses digital marketing assets to attract, engage, and delight customers online. Digital marketing, on the other hand, is simply an umbrella term to describe online marketing tactics of any kind, regardless of whether they're considered inbound or outbound.

Digital marketing is often compared to inbound marketing, but it doesn't differentiate between 'inbound' and 'outbound' methods. It's more of an umbrella term for all marketing that involves digital communication, while inbound marketing is more of a strategy.

Digital outbound tactics put a marketing message in front of as many people as possible online — regardless of whether it's relevant or welcomed. For example, the garish banner ads you see on websites that push a product or promotion to people who aren't necessarily ready to receive it.

Marketers who employ digital inbound tactics use online content to attract their target customers by providing assets that are helpful to them. One of the simplest yet most powerful inbound digital marketing assets is a blog, which allows your website to capitalize on the terms which your ideal customers are searching for.

Does digital marketing work for all businesses?

Digital marketing can work for any business in any industry. Regardless of what your company sells, digital marketing still involves building buyer personas to identify your audience's needs, and creating valuable online content. However, that's not to say all businesses should implement a digital marketing strategy in the same way.

B2B Digital Marketing

If your company is business-to-business (B2B), your digital marketing efforts are likely centered around online lead generation, with the end goal being for someone to speak to a salesperson. The goal of your marketing strategy might be to attract and convert the highest quality leads for your salespeople via your website and to support digital channels.

Beyond your website, you'll probably choose to focus your efforts on business-focused channels like LinkedIn, where your demographic is spending their time online.

B2C Digital Marketing

If your company is business-to-consumer (B2C), depending on the price point of your products, it's likely that the goal of your digital marketing efforts is to attract people to your website and have them become customers without ever needing to speak to a salesperson.

You're probably less likely to focus on ‘leads' in their traditional sense and more likely to build an accelerated buyer's journey from when someone lands on your website to when they make a purchase. This can mean that your product features are higher up in the marketing funnel than it might be for a B2B business, and you might need to use stronger calls-to-action to inspire purchases.

For B2C companies, channels like Instagram, youtube and Pinterest are often more valuable than business-focused platforms like LinkedIn.

What types of digital content should I create?

The kind of content you create depends on your audience's needs at different stages in the buyer's journey. You should start by creating buyer personas to identify what your audience's goals and challenges are in relation to your business. On a basic level, your online content should aim to help them meet these goals, and overcome their challenges.

Then, you'll need to consider when they're most likely to be ready to consume this content in line with their stage in the buyer's journey. We call this content mapping.

With content mapping, the goal is to target content according to:

- The characteristics of the person who will be consuming it (that's where buyer personas come in).
- How close that person is to making a purchase (i.e., their lifecycle stage).

In terms of the format of your content, there are a lot of different things to try. Here are some options we'd recommend using at each stage of the buyer's journey:

a) Awareness Stage

Blog posts. Great for increasing your organic traffic when paired with a strong SEO and keyword strategy.

Infographics. Very shareable, meaning they increase your chances of being found via social media when others share your content.

Short videos. Again, these are very shareable and can help your brand get found by new audiences by hosting them on platforms like YouTube and Pinterest for images.

b) Consideration Stage

Ebooks. Great for lead generation as they're generally more comprehensive than a blog post or infographic, meaning someone is more likely to exchange their contact information to receive it.

Research reports. Again, this high-value content type is great for lead generation. Research reports and new data for your industry can also work for the awareness stage, though, as they're often picked up by the media or industry press.

Webinars. As they're a more detailed, interactive form of video content, webinars are an effective consideration stage content format as they offer more comprehensive content than a blog post or short video.

c) Decision Stage

Case studies. Having detailed case studies on your website can be an effective form of content for those ready to make a purchasing decision, as it helps you positively influence their decision.

Testimonials. If case studies aren't a good fit for your business, having short testimonials around your website is a good alternative. For B2C brands, think of testimonials a little more loosely. If you're a clothing brand, these might take the form of photos of how other people styled a shirt or dress, pulled from a branded hashtag where people can contribute.

8.How to Do Digital Marketing

- Define your goals.
- Identify your target audience.
- Establish a budget for each digital channel.
- Strike a good balance between paid and free digital strategies.
- Create engaging content.
- Optimize your digital assets for mobile.
- Conduct keyword research.
- Iterate based on the analytics you measure.

1. Define your goals.

When you get started with digital marketing, it's critical to identify and define your goals since you'll craft your strategy with them. For instance, if your goal is to increase brand awareness, you might want to focus on reaching new audiences via social media. Or maybe you want to increase sales on a specific product — if that's the case, it's more important you focus on SEO and optimizing content to get potential buyers on your website in the first place. Additionally, if sales are your goal, you might test out PPC campaigns to drive traffic through paid ads. Whatever the case, it's easiest to shape a digital marketing strategy after you've determined your company's biggest goals.

2. Identify your target audience.

We've mentioned this before, but one of the biggest benefits of digital marketing is the opportunity to target specific audiences – however, you can't take advantage of that benefit if you haven't first identified your target audience. Of course, it's important to note your target audience might vary depending on the channel or goal(s) you have for a specific product or campaign. For instance, perhaps you've noticed most of your Instagram audience is younger and prefers funny memes and quick videos — but your LinkedIn audience is older professionals looking for more tactical advice. You'll want to vary your content to appeal to these different target audiences. If you're starting from scratch, feel free to take a look at How to Find Your Target Audience.

3. Establish a budget for each digital channel.

Your budget will depend on the elements of digital marketing you use. If you're focusing on inbound techniques like SEO, social media, and content creation for a pre-existing website, the good news is you don't need a big budget at all. You can aim to create high-quality content your audience will want to consume, where the only investment you'll need is your time.

You can get started by hosting a website and creating content using a CMS. For those on a tight budget, you can get started using WordPress hosted on WP Engine, using a simple theme, and building your site without code using the Elementor Website Builder for WordPress.

With outbound techniques like online advertising and purchasing email lists, there is undoubtedly some expense. What it costs comes down to what kind of visibility you want to receive as a result of the advertising.

For example, to implement PPC using Google AdWords, you'll bid against other companies in your industry to appear at the top of Google's search results for keywords associated with your business. Depending on the keyword's competitiveness, this can be reasonably affordable or could be extremely expensive, which is why it's a good idea to focus on building your organic reach too.

4. Strike good balance between paid & free digital strategies

A digital marketing strategy likely needs both paid and free aspects to truly be effective. For instance, spending time building comprehensive buyer personas to identify your audience's needs and creating high-quality online content that converts them, you'll likely see strong results despite minimal ad spend. However, if paid advertising is part of your digital strategy, then the results might come even quicker. Ultimately, aim to build your organic (or 'free') reach using content, SEO, and social media for more long-term, sustainable success. When in doubt, try both, and iterate on your process as you learn which channels — paid or free – perform best for your brand.

5. Create engaging content.

Once you know your audience and have a budget, it's time to start creating content for the various channels you will use. This content can be social media posts, blog posts, PPC ads, sponsored content, email marketing newsletters, and more. Of course, any content you create should be interesting and engaging to your audience because the point of marketing content is to increase brand awareness and improve lead generation.

6. Optimize your digital assets for mobile.

Another key component of digital marketing is mobile marketing. In fact, smartphone usage as a whole accounts for 69% of time spent consuming digital media in the U.A.E, while desktop-based digital media consumption makes up less than half — and the U A E is mobile's biggest fan compared to other countries.

This means optimize your digital ads, web pages, social media images, and other digital assets for mobile devices is essential. If your company has a mobile app that enables users to engage with your brand or shop for your products, your app falls under the digital marketing umbrella, too.Those engaging with your company mobile devices need to have the same positive experience as they would on a desktop. This means implementing a mobile-friendly or responsive website design to make browsing user-friendly on mobile devices. It might also mean reducing the length of your lead generation forms to create a hassle-free experience for people downloading your content on the go. As for your social media images, it's important to always have a mobile user in mind when creating them, as image dimensions are smaller on mobile devices and text can be cut-off.

There are lots of ways you can optimize your digital marketing assets for mobile users, and when implementing any digital marketing strategy, it's hugely important to consider how the experience will translate on mobile devices. By ensuring this is always front-of-mind, you'll be creating digital experiences that work for your audience, and consequently achieve the results you're hoping for.

7. Conduct keyword research.

Digital marketing is all about reaching targeted audiences through personalized content — all of which can't happen without effective keyword research. Conducting keyword research is critical for optimizing your website and content for SEO and ensuring people can find your business through search engines. Additionally, social media keyword research can also help market your products or services on various social channels. You'll still want to conduct keyword research even if you don't have a full-time SEO strategist. Try creating a list of high-performing keywords related to your products or services, and consider long-tail variations for added opportunities.

8. Iterate based on the analytics you measure.

Finally, to create an effective digital marketing strategy for the long term, it's vital your team learn how to pivot based on analytics.

For instance, perhaps after a couple of months you find your audience isn't as interested in your content on Instagram anymore — but they love what you're creating on Twitter. Sure, this might be an opportunity to re-examine your Instagram strategy as a whole, but it might also be a sign that your audience prefers a different channel to consume branded content.

Alternatively, perhaps you find an older web page isn't getting the traffic it used to. You might consider updating the page or getting rid of it entirely to ensure visitors are finding the freshest, most relevant content for their needs.

Digital marketing provides businesses with incredibly flexible opportunities for continuous growth — but it's up to you to take advantage of them.

I'm ready to try digital marketing. Now what?

If you're already doing digital marketing, you're likely reaching some segments of your audience online. No doubt you can think of some areas of your strategy that could use a little improvement, though.

That's why we created a step-by-step guide to help you build a digital marketing strategy that's truly effective, whether you're a complete beginner or have a little more experience.

Next, let's look at some examples of digital marketing that will be sure to inspire you.

9.Digital Marketing Examples

- Lego's Rebuild the World Campaign
- Dove's Reverse Selfie Campaign
- JenniferLopez's#InTheMorningChallenge
- Always' #DayoftheGirl Campaign
- Topicals - Email Marketing
- Ashley White - Affiliate Marketing
- Samsonite - Search Engine Marketing
- Yes Williamsburg - Sponsored Ad
- Blog - Content Offers
- For Keeps Bookstore - Local Business SEO

1. Lego's Rebuild the World Campaign

Source: Getty images

This is a great example of a digital marketing campaign because it says something about the brand. In this campaign, Lego takes a stance on important global issues as a way to connect with its audience.

Nowadays, it's becoming increasingly important for companies to discuss global issues and show alignment with their customers in that way. The major play of this campaign is to help share the brand's story and messaging.

Given that 82% of customers shop from brands that share their values, this was a good move for the toy brand.

2. Dove's Reverse Selfie Campaign

Source: Getty images

As we continue to learn how social media affects children, especially young girls, Dove decided to send a message. The Reverse Selfie campaign shows the reverse of what a teen girl did to prepare for a selfie and photoshop the picture. The purpose is to increase awareness of how social media can negatively impact self-esteem.

This is an excellent example of what marketing content can look like when you know your audience intimately. By knowing its audience of real women, many of them parents, Dove was able to bring light to an often overlooked consequence of the growth of social media.

3. Jennifer Lopez's #InTheMorningChallenge

In this social media campaign, Jennifer Lopez created a dance challenge to promote her new song. With this challenge, fans would do the same dance in their pajamas and in dress up clothes.

This was a successful social media campaign as the video had over 16 million views and over 5,000 posts.

Using social media is a great way to engage your audience and get them to participate with your brand one on one.

4. Always' #DayoftheGirl Campaign

This is another digital campaign focused on emotional marketing. With this campaign, Always asked their own employees what tips they would give to girls. The women offer their valuable insight in a way meant to inspire everyone for International Day of the Girl, an international holiday that occurs annually in October.

Again, this isn't a campaign where the product is mentioned much, but that isn't the point. The point of this digital campaign was to inspire its audience. With that message, they could reach even more people, increase brand awareness, and show their audience that the brand aligns with their values.

Now we'll look at some examples of different types of digital marketing.

5. Topicals - Email Marketing

Topicals, a skincare company, uses email marketing as part of a digital marketing strategy. The image below displays a marketing email that advertises a subscribe and save deal, where people get 20% off refills if they choose to subscribe.

6. Ashley White - Affiliate Marketing

Ashley White is an esthetician who uses affiliate marketing. In her Twitter profile, she includes a link to a personal Linktree page where she shares referral codes and discounts for people that shop with her codes and links.

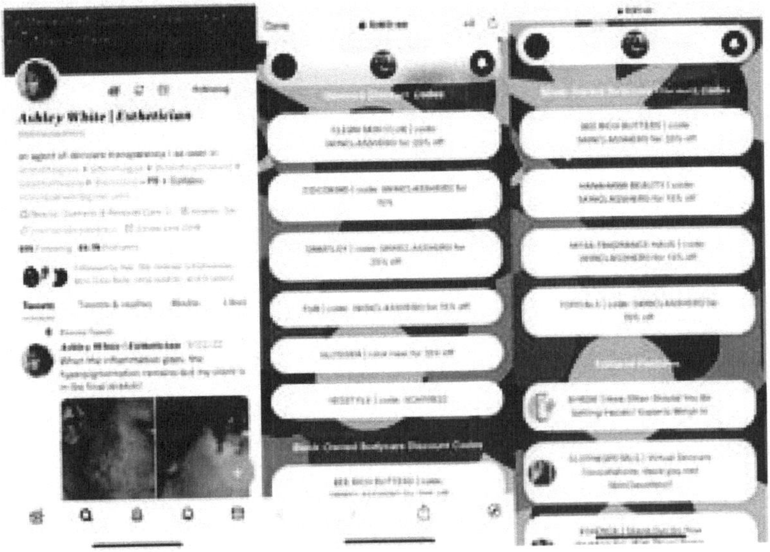

As she markets herself as an ambassador for these companies, the businesses generate brand awareness as someone visiting her Linktree might be inspired to try a new brand (and an influencer recommendation can make this inspiration even more powerful).

7. Samsonite - Search Engine Marketing

Search engine marketing is a great example of digital marketing, where brands bid on keywords and showcase ads for their products in SERPs when someone queries a related keyword.

The image below is an example from Samsonite, where a query for the word "luggage" surfaces various luggage options from known brands that have created ads to feature their products front and center in search results.

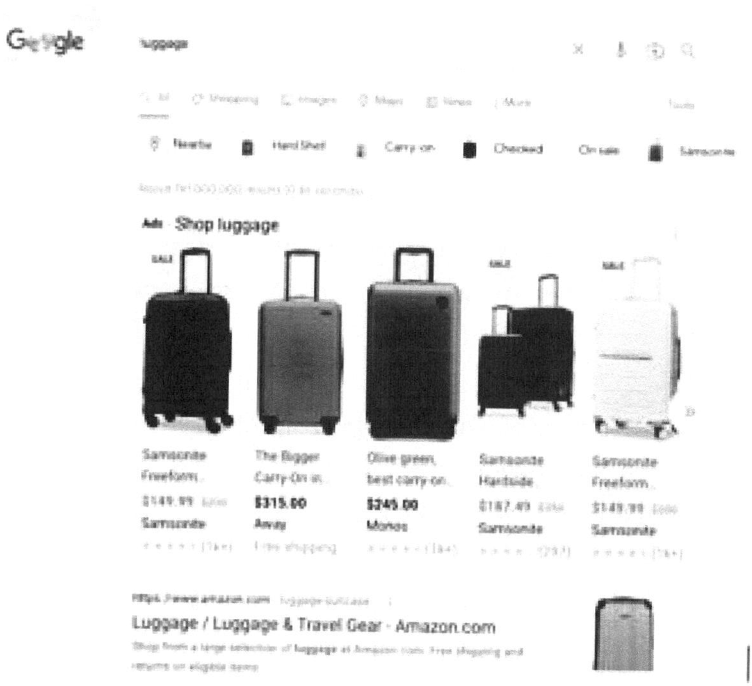

8. Yes Williamsburg - Sponsored Ad

Yes Williamsburg uses native advertising within its Instagram feed to share a paid sponsorship with a local Brooklyn business. The Reel is tagged as a paid partnership, but it appears organically in a users feed like a standard post. The ad is also in line with Yes Williamsbug's usual content of sharing information about unique local businesses for people to try.

9. Blog - Content Offers

Content offers are a form of digital marketing where businesses share helpful content with site visitors that it knows will benefit them. For example, the Blog often features content offers and learning material for people to learn more about the blog topic.

For its blog post 11 Marketing Strategies for Black Owned Businesses, readers that want to know more about developing a marketing strategy can download an ebook for further learning.

10. For Keeps Bookstore - Local Business SEO

A search engine optimization strategy for many local businesses is an optimized Google My Business profile to appear in local search results when people look for products or services related to what you offer. For Keeps Bookstore, a local bookstore in Atlanta, GA, has optimized its Google My Business profile for local SEO so it appears in queries for "atlanta bookstore."

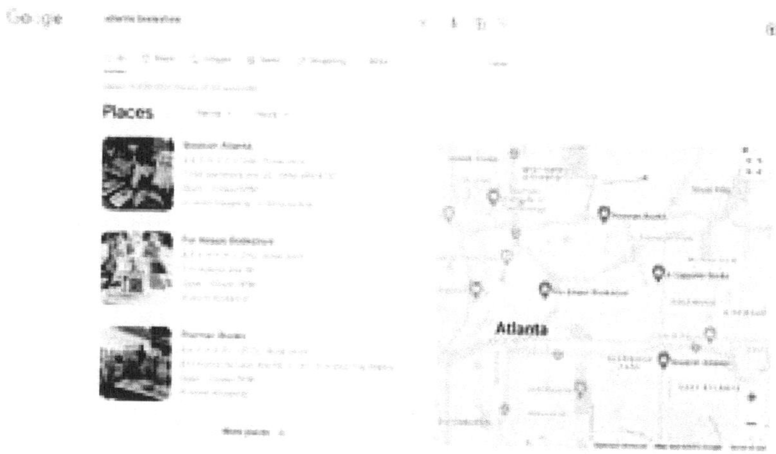

Integrate Digital Marketing Into Your Strategy

Any opportunity where you can connect to your audience is an opportunity to convert a lead or acquire a customer. Digital marketing creates so many more of those opportunities by allowing you to reach prospective buyers through a wide variety of channels. Whether it's social media platforms, websites, text messages, or any online medium, it's an invaluable way to promote your business, service, or product.

10. Treating Your Agency as a Vendor (or Adversary!) Instead of a Partner

When working with an agency, brands often think they can hand over the keys to the castle and never look back. But you need to work with your agency to succeed! Your points of contact at an agency are marketing experts (more on that below), but you are the expert in your brand and business. Therefore, it's only natural that they'll need to pick your brain in order to achieve the highest quality output. If you fall behind on — or even neglect — the review, edit and approval process, you could be a bottleneck to your own success.

The best way to approach a digital marketing agency about runoff work would be to have worked with this agency before, either as an employee or having worked closely with them on the client side, or to get introduced by someone who knows your work and knows a decision maker at the agency.

Source: Getty images

Either of those options automatically takes you out of the pool of "random guys cold-calling hoping for a new client" and fast tracks you to being on the radar of someone who can make a decision as to whether or not to partner with you as a freelancer.

If you can't find any type of connection like that which you or someone in your network can leverage, then your only option is to be one of the random guys cold-calling, hoping to pick up the agency as a new client.

If this is your situation, here are a few recommendations:

- Obviously, if applicable, have a presentation of your company available, so you can make the run through it.

- Much like a content marketer has a persona that influences all of their decisions on targeting, messaging, tone, etc , you should define what type of agencies are most likely to need your services, and what type of agency is most likely to be interested in working with you. If you're well known and a leader in your industry, then pretty much anyone would likely be happy to work with you, but if you don't have a lot of experience or if you've been flying under the radar for the duration of your career, you may have to start out with small to medium sized agencies before you could tackle any big name clients. Focus your time on finding and contacting the agencies that fit that profile.

- Be ready for "No." Some agencies aren't in a place to expand, some already have a relationship with clients and cant take more and are happy with their current partners, some just may not want to work with you. Incorporate the TG and media budget into your pitch.

Also, a bit of advice. But if you're just starting out a new business, I would recommending working in with an agency first. Not only does it help you make those connections that help you get around the usual funnel of people that separate you as an outsider from someone who can actually help you make this partnership happen, but it also teaches you a lot of valuable skills and background knowledge that would make you life much easier.

ISo, to sum it all up. I'd recommend you work within an agency first before becoming their client.I think it would make your life much easier having the experience and connections to help you secure the results you are looking to achieve.

The very best marketing engagements come when the agency and brand are seen as collaborators working towards the same goals.

Source: Getty images

Not Speaking Up

It can be hard to give direct and explicit feedback, especially if you like the manager on your account. But if you don't speak up, how will they know how to improve? Fight the urge to bottle up your opinions and be radically candid at every opportunity (remember that you're the expert in your business, and need to share that knowledge with your new team!). Speak up before you get frustrated and end the engagement.

It is a fact that a digital marketing agency can grow your business fast than most marketing techniques. So talk and get it done! Especially if the agency is fully automated it will rock your ROI through the roof without any follow ups.

- Hiring a digital marketing agency allows you to get started with your campaigns almost immediately. Within 3-5 days is normal to get it right for the digital agency.

- You do not need to navigate the learning curve or set up a team.

- You can see your campaigns live within weeks after creating a strategy. Start by first understanding your needs and sharing them with the agency. And train them about your business, the TG etc.

- Digital Marketing Agencies for business lies in the option to choose your technique of marketing according to your budget and reach a wider audience at a lesser cost.

A digital marketing agency offers a variety of strategies, from SEO, PPC, Content Marketing, Email Marketing, Social Media Marketing, and Voice SEO & Video Marketing, to reach your unique goals. Whether you're looking to increase sales, revenue, awareness, or loyalty.

If you are looking for a digital marketing agency, then Digital Media Sapiens is one of the best digital marketing agencies. as we are fully automated and we believ in provide quality results to its clients. ONTIME, EVERYTIME, JUST LIKE AMAZON.COM.

Source: Getty Images

Forgetting to Align With Your Internal Team

Now you know your agency definitely wants you to speak up. But when you do, it is crucial to present a united front — because we all know what happens when there are too many cooks in the kitchen. So get aligned with your internal team about feedback and plans before letting your agency know how you'd like to proceed. Having this internal alignment from all of the necessary parties on your side of the business in place is key to your agency being able to execute at the highest level possible instead of attempting to execute conflicting campaigns or strategies.

Source: Getty Images

Not Trusting Your Experts to Be Experts

So often agencies suggest strategies that fail to launch based on a client's preconceived notions. Whether it's ignoring an agency's best practices or an unwillingness to experiment, you could be missing out on big opportunities if you're too stuck in your ways or don't trust the expertise of the team that your agency has assembled. Try to put those feelings aside next time you meet with your agency team, and trust that they are employing all of their marketing knowledge and tools to best support your brand's goals.

A digital marketing agency can be a valuable partner to your business, though you may not fully realize all they can do for you. As a sales or marketing manager, your job is to bring in customers through your business' "front doors.

Today, 81 percent of customers conduct online research before making a purchase decision, which means it's imperative to develop a robust online presence that engages and nurtures customers online throughout their customer journey. A digital marketing company can do this for your business, plus a lot more.

Source: Getty Images

Not Giving Your Agency Enough Time

If you've kicked off with an agency in the last quarter and are panicking because of a dip in returns — stop! Take a deep breath, and sit tight. It is so easy to ignore simple things like seasonality and purchase cycles of your customers when looking at returns. It is also easy to forget that digital marketing efforts across nearly all channels have a ramp-up period where your experts will be continually testing and optimizing what works best. Let them do their thing before focusing on returns.

Misreading (or Ignoring!) Data

Collecting data and analytics won't do you any good if you're basing your marketing decisions off of a shaky understanding of the numbers. It is key that you and your agency constantly test, optimize and verify the data that you or Google has collected — doing so will give you a better idea of the overall health of your marketing initiatives and business as a whole.

Once you have a solid understanding of that data, use it as your guiding light. Often brands and agencies clash when the former wants to act off of feelings about the state of their business or the success of their campaigns instead of the numbers. So next time you feel like your engagement with an agency isn't going well, step back and take a look at the numbers — they may just reveal a different story.

Thinking Digital Marketing is a One-Time Game

Digital marketing is (unfortunately) not a one time push. If you've spent money with an agency on marketing and have seen positive results, you can't stop spending and expect those results will continue at the same level. If you're not constantly optimizing and testing old strategies against new ones, you may lose the interest of your new-found audience. Digital evolves fast, and you could be leaving money on the table if you are not constantly updating your messaging, pushing out new creatives and developing new content.

Digital marketing agencies are all-encompassing experts in the industry who can provide opportunities for companies of any size. It is becoming vital that all businesses create a digital presence and use an agency to do it right. People need to be able to find you and have your message stand out in a sea of information that they face each day. A digital marketing expert will help lead you through the maze of different options, as well as provide strategies on how best to approach things like Email Marketing, Paid Search Advertising, Social Media Marketing Services or Online Reputation Management, and more. At a basic level, their expertise means that when companies sign up with one company they don't have to lose hours sifting through the confusing field at SEO, SEM or social media marketing and what is next month on month.

This is expected from the agency brain storming and thinking for your business. Remember- Digital Agency is Turbo

Charging your business and like in any relationship trust is the key factor to make you thrive in 2022.

Poor Communication

The biggest calls of distress we heard from potential clients was poor communication from other agencies they hired. We built our company on this premise. If the agency fails to communicate early on, it will be a disaster going forward.

Lack Of Transparency

Your agency should be open to sharing data, and not after it's filtered through their systems. Expect access to your analytics and AdWords account. Expect straight answers with data and results to back it up. Most importantly, expect truth. Your agency won't always have great news. If things are always sunshine and roses, beware. Things will go wrong and that's OK, with transparency and trust.

Red alert areas you should watch out for from your agency are:

a). Skip Over The Competitive Analysis

Use marketing tools to see how your website is doing versus your competition. If they're doing something right, then find a way to emulate it. If they're doing something wrong, work hard to not make the same mistakes while capitalizing on the opportunity to do a better job. Without this step, you can make costly mistakes that can waste time and even cause you to lose business.

b).Slow Response Time

The majority of the issues business representatives face while dealing with agencies can be attributed to poor communication. A delayed response or team members not being on the same page could signal a lack of organization and many headaches to come. Look for agencies that can present their ideas and processes clearly before they unleash their creative flair.

c). How They Promote Themselves

This is an important question to consider. I have seen agencies focused on promoting their business more effectively through communication tactics than the clients they represent. Be wary of a firm's veneer and how they present themselves. If they come first, it's a red flag!

d).They Say They Can Do Everything

Small agencies that say they can do everything may or may not be able to, but usually at a high risk. If it's a small agency, one employee may do many things very well, but if they leave, it can throw your business off-track. Protect yourself by looking on LinkedIn to see how much depth of expertise they have. If they have eight specialty areas and six employees, it should be a huge red flag.

e). They Promise Specific Results and they don't show any data of Google Analytics, Web master tool, Facebook Analytics etc.

Any agency that promises you specific results is just trying to get you through the door. There is no secret sauce to marketing, it's all about testing and finding what works best for each client. You can absolutely pull learnings from past clients and test them with current clients, but in no way does that guarantee positive results. If an agency is promising you the world, kindly decline

Now we will dive deep into each subject of the core understanding of each service and how it could help you in your business.

What is performance marketing?

Performance-based advertising, also known as pay for performance advertising, is a form of advertising in which the purchaser pays only when there are measurable results. Performance-based advertising is becoming more common with the spread of electronic media, notably the Internet, where it is possible to measure user actions resulting from advertisement. Performance Marketing is different from Brand Marketing which focuses on awareness, consideration, and opinions among target consumers.

Performance marketing is mere numbers-

1. Number of visitors on your website,
2. Number of times they visit your website,
3. Number of new visitors daily,
4. Number of minutes they spend on your website,
5. Number of clicks on your ads,
6. Number of visitors visiting your website from the ads (paid medium),
7. Number of visitors buying your product,
8. Number of revenue,
9. Cost per conversion,
10. Cost per acquisition,
11. Cost per client.

So You are aware as to, how many clients you are getting from each segment-

1. The numbers you get from paid,
2. The numbers from owned and
3. The number from earned mediums
4. Cost per conversion.

And we at Digital Media Sapiens guarantee 300% ROI on the media budget spent, out of which at least 20%-30% qualified leads should convert, which can vary depending on your business vertical and if you are start up e-commerce which could be an exception as e-commerce business needs a lot of time depending on the ticket value . Our team focus is Improving numbers every day, every hour should be the commitment of all the digital marketing agencies - Digital Marketing Managers and the team.

There are four common costing models used in the online performance advertising market.

1. CPM (cost-per-mille, or cost-per-thousand) pricing models charge advertisers for impressions, i.e. the number of times people view an advertisement. Display advertising is commonly sold on a CPM pricing model. The problem with CPM advertising is that advertisers are charged even if the target audience does not click on the advertisement.

2. CPC (cost-per-click) advertising overcomes this problem by charging advertisers only when the consumer clicks on the advertisement. However, due to increased competition, search keywords have become very expensive. Doubleclick Performics Search Trends Report shows that there were nearly six times as many keywords with a cost per click (CPC) of more than Dhs 3.68 in January 2022 than the prior year. The cost per keyword increased by 33% and the cost per click rose by as much as 55%. In recent times, there has been a rapid increase in online lead generation – banner and direct response advertising that works off a CPL pricing model. In a cost-per-lead pricing model, advertisers pay only for qualified leads – irrespective of the clicks or impressions that went into generating the lead. CPL advertising is also commonly referred to as online lead generation.

3. Cost per lead (CPL) pricing models are the most advertiser friendly. A recent IBM research study found that two-thirds of senior marketers expect 20 percent of ad revenue to move away from impression-based sales, in favor of action-based models within three years. CPL models allow advertisers to pay only for qualified leads as opposed to clicks or impressions and are at the pinnacle of the online advertising ROI hierarchy.

4. In CPA advertising, or Cost Per Acquisition, advertisers pay for a specific action such as a credit card transaction (also called CPO, cost-per-order).

Advertisers need to be careful when choosing between CPL and CPA pricing models.

In CPL campaigns, advertisers pay for an interested lead – i.e. the contact information of a person interested in the advertiser's product or service. CPL campaigns are suitable for brand marketers and direct response marketers looking to engage consumers at multiple touch-points – by building a newsletter list, community site, reward program or member acquisition program.

In CPA campaigns, the advertiser typically pays for a completed sale involving a credit card transaction. CPA is all about 'now' – it focuses on driving consumers to buy at that exact moment. If a visitor to the website doesn't buy anything, there's no easy way to re-market to them.

There are other important differentiators:

- CPL campaigns are advertiser-centric. The advertiser remains in control of their brand, selecting trusted and contextually relevant publishers to run their offers. On the other hand, CPA and affiliate marketing campaigns are publisher-centric. Advertisers cede control over where their brand will appear, as publishers browse offers and pick which to run on their websites. Advertisers generally do not know where their offer is running.

- CPL campaigns are usually high volume and light-weight. In CPL campaigns, consumers submit only basic contact information. The transaction can be as simple as an email address. On the other hand, CPA campaigns are usually low-volume and complex. Typically, consumers have to submit credit cards and other detailed information.

- CPL advertising is more appropriate for advertisers looking to deploy acquisition campaigns by re-marketing to end consumers through e-newsletters, community sites, reward programs, loyalty programs, and other engagement vehicles.

Metrics

Various types of measurable action may be used in charging for performance-based advertising:

- Many Digital and social platforms charge for advertising on a "CPM" (cost per thousand) or cost per impression basis. That is, the advertiser pays only when a consumer sees their advertisement. Some would argue that this is not performance-based advertising since there is no measurement of the user response.

- Internet sites often also offer advertising on a "PPC" (pay per click) basis. Google's AdWords product and equivalent products from Millennial Media, Yahoo!, Microsoft , and others support PPC advertising plans.

- A small but growing number of sites are starting to offer plans on a "Pay per call" basis. The user can click a button to place a VoIP call, or to request a call from the advertiser. If the user requests a call, presumably they are highly likely to make a purchase.

- Finally, there is considerable research into methods of linking the user's actions to the eventual purchase: the ideal form of performance measurement.

Some Internet sites are markets, bringing together buyers and sellers. eBay, Amazon are a prominent example of a market operating on an auction basis. Other market sites let the vendors set their price. In either model, the market mediates sales and takes a commission – a defined percentage of the sale value. The market is motivated to give a more prominent position to vendors who achieve high sales value. Markets may be seen as a form of performance-based advertising.

The use of mobile coupons also enables a whole new world of metrics within identifying campaign effect. There are several providers of mobile coupon technology that makes it possible to provide unique coupons or barcodes to each individual person and at the same time identify the person downloading it. This makes it possible to follow these individuals during the whole process from downloading until when and where the coupons are redeemed.

What is SEO?

S.E.O. is Search Engine Optimization, that means the google bots are crawling on your website and how they are seeing your website and that they are forming an interpretation of your website appears to the bots. And google machine crawling on your website ranks you on the ratings and guidelines set by Google through Penguin and Panda updates. There are many criterias starting with page speed and loading time of the website. And the new core vital update of Google in 2022 giving priority to the user experience, the content quality, impact and uniqueness launched in the year 2022. There are two types of S.E.O., one is focused on E- Commerce, which is basically sales-oriented numbers, revenue generated and then there is SEO which is lead generation and is meant for the corporate websites with contact us form. We have to optimize the websites, so that it's Google bot crawlable. It's like indexing the content of a book. We have to “inform" Google what to crawl means what to see on the website and what not to crawl and google understands only the English Language. Therefore, we have to tag every single image on our website with text in English so that Google can know what the image is depicting. And then for backlinking seo juice, one has to create monthly atleast 4 blogs for a basic website with 20 plus pages and 10-20 per month for website over 500 pages to get any interaction, which are recommended and website content page for each keyword we are targeting because if you are the Burj Khalifa or you are a 3 star hotel, google doesn't know it is just number of visitors, links on your website makes you conducive to leads and sales.

So, how big you are depends on the pages, links, clicks, form fills. We need to create an apt content which is dynamic, impactful and attention stimulating. And apart from this, we need to use our content on YouTube plus all social media channels - owned, earned and paid media, relative to our audiences, in demand. And from this content which is shared by blogs on different forums, websites and blogs in both Arabic and English or now in UAE with 180 nationalities, we also have Russian and Chinese. This helps your potential customers to get to your website, and we can target services your clients are looking for your solutions to your website form and then we entice them to at least more than 2 minutes on your website as per the Google algorithm crawl standards to rank you above your competition. Additionally, if the bounce rate is very low, if the content quality, the English attribute to the value which you offer to your clients. If everyone loves you, Google loves you too. And this love will result in you on TOP, Google will rank you on top of your competitors. Not to mention that every quarterly it is important to audit your website compared to your competitors on position 1 on 1st page of Google. Content gap analysis is the key. So the idea is you are ahead of your competitors and be on position 1 on the 1st page of Google.

There are two types of S.E.O., which is E- Commerce, which is basically sales oriented and there is second type which is most common is lead generation/form filling which is basically for the corporate websites. So, what we have to optimize the websites, so that it's Google crawlable, its like indexing. It's like the index of a book.

We have to navigate and inform Google- where and what to see/crawl, what not to see/crawl and Google understands only the English language. We have to image tag every single image on your website, so that Google can know what is the image all about and then we have to create blogs and content, because if you are Burj Khalifa or you are a 3 star hotel, google doesn't know and you know, that how big you are so we need to create a lot of content and from this content which is shared on blogs and on different forums, in Arabic and English mainly plus Russian, Chinese, Hindi etc. we bring back SEO juice or all the online customers looking for your services to your website and the job is done with form filling. Then is the job of your sales representative to convert.

Search engine optimization (SEO) is the process of improving the quality and quantity of the website traffic to a website or a web page from search engines. SEO targets unpaid traffic (known as "natural" or "organic" results) rather than direct traffic or paid traffic. Unpaid traffic may originate from different kinds of searches, including image search, video search, academic search, news search, and industry-specific vertical search engines.

As an Internet marketing strategy, SEO considers how search engines works, the computer-programmed algorithms that dictate search engine behavior, what people search for, the actual search terms or keywords typed into search engines, and which search engines are preferred by their targeted audience. SEO is performed because a website will receive more visitors from a search engine when websites rank higher on the search engine results page (SERP). These visitors can then potentially be converted into customers.

Webmasters and content providers began optimizing websites for search engines, as the first search engines were cataloging the early Web. Initially, all webmasters only needed to submit the address of a page, or URL, to the various engines, which would send a web crawler to crawl that page, extract links to other pages from it, and return information found on the page to be indexed.. The process involves a search engine spider downloading a page and storing it on the search engine's own server. A second program, known as an indexer, extracts information about the page, such as the words it contains, where they are located, and any weight for specific words, as well as all links the page contains. All of this information is then placed into a scheduler for crawling at a later date.

Website owners recognized the value of a high ranking and visibility in search engine results,. creating an opportunity for both white-hat and black-hat SEO practitioners. According to industry analyst Danny Sullivan, the phrase "search engine optimization" probably came into use in 1997. Sullivan credits Bruce Clay as one of the first people to popularize the term..

Early versions of search algorithms relied on webmaster-provided information such as the keyword meta tag or index files in engines like ALIWEB. Meta tags provide a guide to each page's content. Using metadata to index pages was found to be less than reliable, however, because the webmaster's choice of keywords in the meta tag could potentially be an inaccurate representation of the site's actual content.

Flawed data in meta tags, such as those that were not accurate, complete, or falsely attributes, created the potential for pages to be mischaracterized in irrelevant searches..[dubious – discuss] Web content providers also manipulated some attributes within the HTML source of a page in an attempt to rank well in search engines.. By 1997, search engine designers recognized that webmasters were making efforts to rank well in their search engine and that some webmasters were even manipulating their rankings in search results by stuffing pages with excessive or irrelevant keywords. Early search engines, such as Altavista and Infoseek, adjusted their algorithms to prevent webmasters from manipulating rankings.

By heavily relying on factors such as keyword density, which were exclusively within a webmaster's control, early search engines suffered from abuse and ranking manipulation. To provide better results to their users, search engines had to adapt to ensure their results pages showed the most relevant search results, rather than unrelated pages stuffed with numerous keywords by unscrupulous webmasters. This meant moving away from heavy reliance on term density to a more holistic process for scoring semantic signals.

Since the success and popularity of a search engine are determined by its ability to produce the most relevant results to any given search, poor quality or irrelevant search results could lead users to find other search sources.

Search engines responded by developing more complex ranking algorithms, taking into account additional factors that were more difficult for webmasters to manipulate.

Companies that employ overly aggressive techniques can get their client websites banned from the search results. In 2005, the Wall Street Journal reported on a company, Traffic Power, which allegedly used high-risk techniques and failed to disclose those risks to its clients.. Wired magazine reported that the same company sued blogger and SEO Aaron Wall for writing about the ban.. Google's Matt Cutts later confirmed that Google did in fact ban Traffic Power and some of its clients..

Some search engines have also reached out to the SEO industry and are frequent sponsors and guests at SEO conferences, webchats, and seminars. Major search engines provide information and guidelines to help with website optimization... Google has a Sitemaps program to help webmasters learn if Google is having any problems indexing their website and also provides data on Google traffic to the website.. Bing Webmaster Tools provides a way for webmasters to submit a sitemap and web feeds, allows users to determine the "crawl rate," and track the web pages index status.

In 2015, it was reported that Google was developing and promoting mobile search as a key feature within future products. In response, many brands began to take a different approach to their Internet marketing strategies..

Relationship with Google

In 1998, two graduate students at Stanford University, Larry Page and Sergey Brin, developed "Backrub," a search engine that relied on a mathematical algorithm to rate the prominence of web pages. The number calculated by the algorithm, Page Rank, is a function of the quantity and strength of inbound links.. PageRank estimates the likelihood that a given page will be reached by a web user who randomly surfs the web, and follows links from one page to another. In effect, this means that some links are stronger than others, as a higher PageRank page is more likely to be reached by the random web surfer.

Page and Brin founded Google in 1998.. Google attracted a loyal following among the growing number of Internet users, who liked its simple design.. Off-page factors (such as Page Rank and hyperlink analysis) were considered as well as on-page factors (such as keyword frequency, meta tags, headings, links and site structure) to enable Google to avoid the kind of manipulation seen in search engines that only considered on-page factors for their rankings.

Although PageRank was more difficult to game, webmasters had already developed link-building tools and schemes to influence the Inktomi search engine, and these methods proved similarly applicable to gaming PageRank. Many sites focus on exchanging, buying, and selling links, often on a massive scale. Some of these schemes, or link farms, involved the creation of thousands of sites for the sole purpose of link spamming..

By 2004, search engines had incorporated a wide range of undisclosed factors in their ranking algorithms to reduce the impact of link manipulation. In June 2007, The New York Times' Saul Hansell stated Google ranks sites using more than 200 different signals.. The leading search engines, Google, Bing, and Yahoo, do not disclose the algorithms they use to rank pages. Some SEO practitioners have studied different approaches to search engine optimization and have shared their personal opinions.. Patents related to search engines can provide information to better understand search engines.. In 2005, Google began personalizing search results for each user. Depending on their history of previous searches, Google crafted results for logged in users..

In 2007, Google announced a campaign against paid links that transfer PageRank.. On June 15, 2009, Google disclosed that they had taken measures to mitigate the effects of PageRank sculpting by use of the no-follow attribute on links. Matt Cutts, a well-known software engineer at Google, announced that Google Bot would no longer treat any no-follow links in the same way to prevent SEO service providers from using no follow for PageRank sculpting. As a result of this change, the usage of no-follow led to the evaporation of PageRank. In order to avoid the above, SEO engineers developed alternative techniques that replace non-followed tags with obfuscated JavaScript and thus permit PageRank sculpting. Additionally, several solutions have been suggested that include the usage of iframes, Flash, and JavaScript.

In December 2009, Google announced it would be using the web search history of all its users in order to populate search results. On June 8, 2010, a new web indexing system called Google Caffeine was announced. Designed to allow users to find news results, forum posts, and other content much sooner after publishing than before, Google Caffeine was a change to the way Google updated its index in order to make things show up quicker on Google than before. According to Carrie Grimes, the software engineer who announced Caffeine for Google, "Caffeine provides 50 percent fresher results for web searches than our last index...". Google Instant, real-time-search, was introduced in late 2010 in an attempt to make search results more timely and relevant. Historically site administrators have spent months or even years optimizing a website to increase search rankings. With the growth in popularity of social media sites and blogs, the leading engines made changes to their algorithms to allow fresh content to rank quickly within the search results.

In February 2011, Google announced the Panda update, which penalizes websites containing content duplicated from other websites and sources. Historically, websites have copied content from one another and benefited in search engine rankings by engaging in this practice. However, Google implemented a new system that punishes sites whose content is not unique.. The 2012 Google Penguin attempted to penalize websites that used manipulative techniques to improve their rankings on the search engine.. Although Google Penguin has been presented as an algorithm aimed at fighting web spam, it really focuses on spammy links.

by gauging the quality of the sites the links are coming from. The 2013 Google Hummingbird update featured an algorithm change designed to improve Google's natural language processing and semantic understanding of web pages.

Hummingbird's language processing system falls under the newly recognized term of "conversational search," where the system pays more attention to each word in the query in order to better match the pages to the meaning of the query rather than a few words. With regards to the changes made to search engine optimization, for content publishers and writers, Hummingbird is intended to resolve issues by getting rid of irrelevant content and spam, allowing Google to produce high-quality content and rely on them to be 'trusted' authors.

In October 2019, Google announced they would start applying BERT models for English language search queries in the US. Bidirectional Encoder Representations from Transformers (BERT) was another attempt by Google to improve their natural language processing, but this time in order to better understand the search queries of their users.. In terms of search engine optimization, BERT intended to connect users more easily to relevant content and increase the quality of traffic coming to websites that are ranking in the Search Engine Results Page.

Metrics

a) Getting indexed

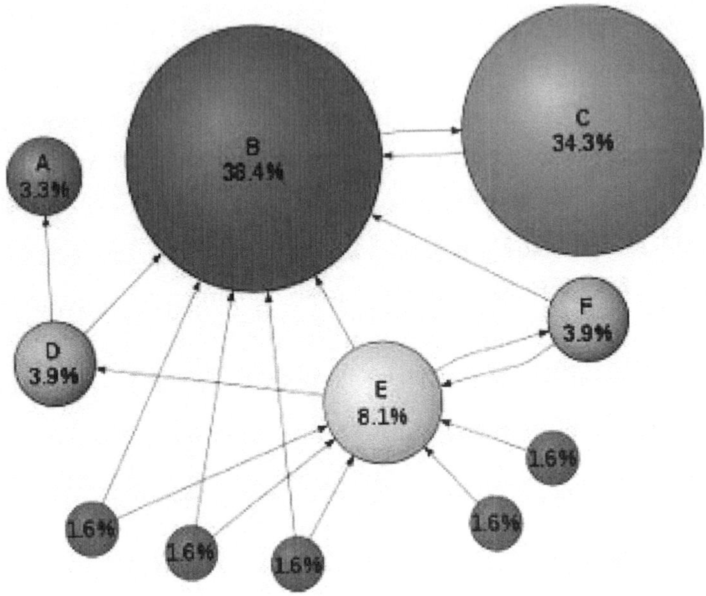

Search engines use complex mathematical algorithms to interpret which websites a user seeks. In this diagram, where each bubble represents a website, programs sometimes called spiders examine which sites link to which other sites, with arrows representing these links. Websites getting more inbound links, or stronger links, are presumed to be more important and what the user is searching for. In this example, since website B is the recipient of numerous inbound links, it ranks more highly in a web search. And the links "carry through", such that website C, even though it only has one inbound link, has an inbound link from a highly popular site (B) while site E does not.

Note: Percentages are rounded.

The leading search engines, such as Google, Bing, and Yahoo!, use crawlers to find pages for their algorithmic search results.

Pages that are linked from other search engine-indexed pages do not need to be submitted because they are found automatically. The Yahoo! Directory and DMOZ, two major directories which closed in 2014 and 2017 respectively, both required manual submission and human editorial review.. Google offers Google Search Console, for which an XML Sitemap feed can be created and submitted for free to ensure that all pages are found, especially pages that are not discoverable by automatically following links. in addition to their URL submission console.. Yahoo! formerly operated a paid submission service that guaranteed to crawl for a cost per click;. however, this practice was discontinued.

Search engine crawlers may look at a number of different factors when crawling a site. Not every page is indexed by search engines. The distance of pages from the root directory of a site may also be a factor in whether or not pages get crawled.

Today, most people are searching on Google using a mobile device.. In November 2021, Google announced a major change to the way crawling websites and started to make its index mobile-first, which means the mobile version of a given website becomes the starting point for what Google includes in its index.

In May 2021, Google updated the rendering engine of their crawler to be the latest version of Chromium (74 at the time of the announcement). Google indicated that they would regularly update the Chromium rendering engine to the latest version.. In December, again, Google began updating the User-Agent string of their crawler to reflect the latest Chrome version used by their rendering service. The delay was to allow webmasters time to update their code that responded to particular bot User-Agent strings. Google ran evaluations and felt confident the impact would be minor.

b) Preventing crawling

To avoid undesirable content in the search indexes, webmasters can instruct spiders not to crawl certain files or directories through the standard robots.txt file in the root directory of the domain. Additionally, a page can be explicitly excluded from a search engine's database by using a meta tag specific to robots (usually <meta name="robots" content="noindex">). When a search engine visits a site, the robots.txt located in the root directory is the first file crawled. The robots.txt file is then parsed and will instruct the robot as to which pages are not to be crawled.

As a search engine crawler may keep a cached copy of this file, it may on occasion crawl pages a webmaster does not wish to crawl. Pages typically prevented from being crawled include login-specific pages such as shopping carts and user-specific content such as search results from internal searches.

In March 2007, Google warned webmasters that they should prevent indexing of internal search results because those pages are considered search spam.. In 2020 Google sunsetted the standard (and open-sourced their code) and now treats it as a hint not a directive. To adequately ensure that pages are not indexed, a page-level robot's meta tag should be included..

c) Increasing prominence

A variety of methods can increase the prominence of a webpage within the search results. Cross-linking between pages of the same website to provide more links to important pages may improve its visibility. Page design makes users trust a site and want to stay once they find it. When people bounce off a site, it counts against the site and affects their credibility. Writing content that includes frequently searched keyword phrases so as to be relevant to a wide variety of search queries will tend to increase traffic. Updating content so as to keep search engines crawling back frequently can give additional weight to a site. Adding relevant keywords to a web page's metadata, including the title tag and meta description, will tend to improve the relevancy of a site's search listings, thus increasing traffic. URL canonicalization of web pages accessible via multiple URLs, using the canonical link element. or via 301 redirects can help make sure links to different versions of the URL all count towards the page's link popularity score. These are known as incoming links, which point to the URL and can count towards the page link's popularity score, impacting the credibility of a website.

Also, in recent times Google has given more priority to the below elements for SERP (Search Engine Ranking Position).

- HTTPS version (Secure Site)
- Page Speed
- Structured Data
- Mobile Compatibility
- AMP (Accelerated Mobile Pages)
- BERT
- Core Vital Updates

d) White hat versus black hat techniques

SEO techniques can be classified into two broad categories: techniques that search engine companies recommend as part of good design ("white hat"), and those techniques of which search engines do not approve ("black hat"). The search engines attempt to minimize the effect of the latter, among them spamdexing. Industry commentators have classified these methods and the practitioners who employ them as either white hat SEO or black hat SEO.. White hats tend to produce results that last a long time, whereas black hats anticipate that their sites may eventually be banned either temporarily or permanently once the search engines discover what they are doing.

An SEO technique is considered a white hat if it conforms to the search engines' guidelines and involves no deception. As the search engine guidelines... are not written as a series of rules or commandments, this is an important distinction to note.

White hat SEO is not just about following guidelines but is about ensuring that the content a search engine indexes and subsequently ranks is the same content a user will see. White hat advice is generally summed up as creating content for users, not for search engines, and then making that content easily accessible to the online "spider" algorithms, rather than attempting to trick the algorithm from its intended purpose.

White hat SEO is in many ways similar to web development that promotes accessibility,. although the two are not identical. Black hat SEO attempts to improve rankings in ways that are disapproved of by the search engines or involve deception. One black hat technique uses hidden text, either as text colored similar to the background, in an invisible div, or positioned off-screen. Another method gives a different page depending on whether the page is being requested by a human visitor or a search engine, a technique known as cloaking. Another category sometimes used is grey hat SEO. This is in between the black hat and white hat approaches, where the methods employed avoid the site being penalized but do not act in producing the best content for users. Grey hat SEO is entirely focused on improving search engine rankings.

Search engines may penalize sites they discover using black or grey hat methods, either by reducing their rankings or by eliminating their listings from their databases altogether. Such penalties can be applied either automatically by the search engines' algorithms or by a manual site review. One example was the February 2006 Google removal of both BMW Germany and Ricoh Germany for the use of deceptive practices.. Both companies, however, quickly apologized, fixed the offending pages, and were restored to Google's search engine results page.

As a marketing strategy, SEO is not an appropriate strategy for every website, and other Internet marketing strategies can be more effective, such as paid advertising through pay-per-click (PPC) campaigns, depending on the site operator's goals. Search engine marketing (SEM) is the practice of designing, running, and optimizing search engine ad campaigns. Its difference from SEO is most simply depicted as the difference between paid and unpaid priority ranking in search results. SEM focuses on prominence more so than relevance; website developers should regard SEM with the utmost importance with consideration to visibility as most navigate to the primary listings of their search.. A successful Internet marketing campaign may also depend upon building high-quality web pages to engage and persuade Internet users, setting up analytics programs to enable site owners to measure results, and improving a site's conversion rate.. In November 2015, Google released a full 160-page version of its Search Quality Rating Guidelines to the public,. which revealed a shift in their focus towards "usefulness" and mobile local search. In recent years the mobile market has exploded, overtaking the use of desktops, as shown in by StatCounter in October 2016, where they analyzed 2.5 million websites and found that 51.3% of the pages were loaded by a mobile device.. Google has been one of the companies that are utilizing the popularity of mobile usage by encouraging websites to use their Google Search Console, the Mobile-Friendly Test, which allows companies to measure up their website to the search engine results and determine how user-friendly their websites are. The closer the keywords are together, their ranking will improve based on key terms.

SEO may generate an adequate return on investment. However search engines are not paid for organic search traffic, their algorithms change, and there are no guarantees of continued referrals. Due to this lack of guarantee and the uncertainty, a business that relies heavily on search engine traffic can suffer major losses if the search engines stop sending visitors.. Search engines can change their algorithms, impacting a website's search engine ranking, possibly resulting in a serious loss of traffic. According to Google's CEO, Eric Schmidt, in 2010, Google made over 500 algorithm changes – almost 1.5 per day. It is considered a wise business practice for website operators to liberate themselves from dependence on search engine traffic. In addition to accessibility in terms of web crawlers (addressed above), the user web accessibility has become increasingly important for SEO.

e) International market

Optimization techniques are highly tuned to the dominant search engines in the target market. The search engines' market shares vary from market to market, as does competition. In 2003, Danny Sullivan stated that Google represented about 75% of all searches. In markets outside the United States, Google's share is often larger, and Google remains the most dominant search engine worldwide as of 2007. As of 2006, Google had an 85–90% market share in Germany.. While there were hundreds of SEO firms in the US at that time, there were only about five in Germany. As of June 2008, the market share of Google in the UK was close to 90% according to Hitwise. That market share is achieved in a number of countries.

As of 2009, there are only a few large markets where Google is not the leading search engine. In most cases, when Google is not leading in a given market, it is lagging behind a local player. The most notable example markets are China, Japan, South Korea, Russia, and the Czech Republic, where respectively Baidu, Yahoo! Japan, Naver, Yandex and Seznam are market leaders.

Successful search optimization for international markets may require professional translation of web pages, registration of a domain name with a top-level domain in the target market, and web hosting that provides a local IP address. Otherwise, the fundamental elements of search optimization are essentially the same, regardless of language.

Search engine marketing (SEM) is a form of internet marketing that involves the promotion of websites by increasing their visibility in search engine results pages (SERPs) primarily through paid advertising. SEM may incorporate search engine optimization (SEO), which adjusts or rewrites website content and site architecture to achieve a higher ranking in search engine results pages to enhance pay-per-click (PPC) listings and increase the Call to action (CTA) on the website.

SEM Elaborated

1 Market
2 History
3 Methods and metrics
4 Paid inclusion
5 Comparison with SEO
6 Ethical questions

1. Market

U.A. E advertisers spent US $2.6 billion like 10 years ago on search engine marketing. Google (73.7%) and the Yahoo/Bing (26.3%) partnership accounted for almost 100% of U.A.E.. search engine spend..
As of 2022, SEM was growing much faster than traditional advertising and even other channels of online marketing.. Managing search campaigns is either done directly with the SEM vendor or through an SEM tool provider. It may also be self-serve or through an advertising agency.

As of today,, Google leads the global search engine market with a market share of 89.3%. Bing comes second with a market share of 4.36%, Yahoo comes third with a market share of 3.3%, and Chinese search engine Baidu is fourth globally with a share of about 0.68%..

Search Engine marketing is also a method of business analytics, which is mainly aimed to provide useful information for organizations to find business opportunity and generate profits. SEM can help organizations to optimize their marketing and gather more audience and create more customers.

2. History

As the number of sites on the Web increased in the mid-to-late 2000, search engines started appearing to help people find information quickly. Search engines developed business models to finance their services, such as pay per click programs offered by Open Text. In 1996 and then Goto.com. in 1998. Goto.com later changed its name. to Overture in 2001, was purchased by Yahoo! in 2003, and now offers paid search opportunities for advertisers through Yahoo! Search Marketing. Google also began to offer advertisements on search results pages in 2000 through the Google AdWords program. By 2007, pay-per-click programs proved to be primary moneymakers. for search engines. In a market dominated by Google, in 2009 Yahoo! and Microsoft announced the intention to forge an alliance. The Yahoo! & Microsoft Search Alliance eventually received approval from regulators in the US and Europe in February 2010..

Search engine optimization consultants expanded their offerings to help businesses learn about and use the advertising opportunities offered by search engines, and new agencies focusing primarily upon marketing and advertising through search engines emerged. The term "search engine marketing" was popularized by Danny Sullivan in 2001. to cover the spectrum of activities involved in performing SEO, managing paid listings at the search engines, submitting sites to directories, and developing online marketing strategies for businesses, organizations, and individuals.

3. Methods and metrics

Search engine marketing uses at least five methods and metrics to optimize websites.

1. Keyword research and analysis involve three "steps": ensuring the site can be indexed in the search engines, finding the most relevant and popular keywords for the site and its products, and using those keywords on the site in a way that will generate and convert traffic. A follow-on effect of keyword analysis and research is the search perception impact. Search perception impact describes the identified impact of a brand's search results on consumer perception, including title and meta tags, site indexing, and keyword focus. As online searching is often the first step for potential consumers/customers, the search perception impact shapes the brand impression for each individual.

2. Website saturation and popularity, or how much presence a website has on search engines, can be analyzed through the number of pages of the site that are indexed by search engines (saturation) and how many backlinks the site has (popularity). It requires pages to contain keywords people are looking for and ensure that they rank high enough in search engine rankings. Most search engines include some form of link popularity in their ranking algorithms. The following are major tools measuring various aspects of saturation and link popularity: Link Popularity, Top 10 Google Analysis, and Marketleap's Link Popularity and Search Engine Saturation.

3. Back-end tools, including Web analytic tools and HTML validators, provide data on a website and its visitors and allow the success of a website to be measured. They range from simple traffic counters to tools that work with log files and to more sophisticated tools that are based on page tagging (putting JavaScript or an image on a page to track actions). These tools can deliver conversion-related information. Validators check the invisible parts of websites, highlighting potential problems and many usability issues and ensuring websites meet W3C code standards. Try to use more than one HTML validator or spider simulator because each one tests, highlights, and reports on slightly different aspects of your website.

4. Whois tools reveal the owners of various websites and can provide valuable information relating to copyright and trademark issues.

5. Google Mobile-Friendly Website Checker: This test will analyze a URL and report if the page has a mobile-friendly design.

Search engine marketing is a way to create and edit a website so that search engines rank it higher than other pages. It should be also focused on keyword marketing or pay-per-click advertising (PPC). The technology enables advertisers to bid on specific keywords or phrases and ensures ads appear with the results of search engines.

With the development of this system, from then till 2022 the price is growing under a high level of competition. Many advertisers prefer to expand their activities, including increasing search engines and adding more keywords. The more advertisers are willing to pay for clicks, the higher the ranking for advertising, which leads to higher traffic.. PPC comes at a cost. The higher position is likely to cost $5 for a given keyword, and $4.50 for a third location. A third advertiser earns 10% less than the top advertiser while reducing traffic by 50%..

Investors must consider their return on investment when engaging in PPC campaigns. Buying traffic via PPC will deliver a positive ROI when the total cost-per-click for a single conversion remains below the profit margin. That way the amount of money spent to generate revenue is below the actual revenue generated.

There are many reasons explaining why advertisers choose the SEM strategy. First, creating a SEM account is easy and can build traffic quickly based on the degree of competition. The shopper who uses the search engine to find information tends to trust and focus on the links showed in the results pages.

However, a large number of online sellers do not buy search engine optimization to obtain higher ranking lists of search results but prefer paid links. A growing number of online publishers are allowing search engines such as Google to crawl content on their pages and place relevant ads on it..

From an online seller's point of view, this is an extension of the payment settlement and an additional incentive to invest in paid advertising projects. Therefore, it is virtually impossible for advertisers with limited budgets to maintain the highest rankings in the increasingly competitive search market.

Google's search engine marketing is one of the western world's marketing leaders, while its search engine marketing is its biggest source of profit.. Google's search engine providers are clearly ahead of the Yahoo and Bing network. The display of unknown search results is free, while advertisers are willing to pay for each click of the ad in the sponsored search results.

4. Paid inclusion

Paid inclusion involves a search engine company charging fees for the inclusion of a website in their results pages. Also known as sponsored listings, paid inclusion products are provided by most search engine companies either in the main results area or as a separately identified advertising area.

The fee structure is both a filter against superfluous submissions and a revenue generator. Typically, the fee covers an annual subscription for one webpage, which will automatically be cataloged on a regular basis. However, some companies are experimenting with non-subscription-based fee structures where purchased listings are displayed permanently. A per-click fee may also apply.

Each search engine is different. Some sites allow only paid inclusion, although these have had little success.

More frequently, many search engines, like Yahoo!,. mix paid inclusion (per-page and per-click fee) with results from web crawling. Others, like Google (and as of 2006, Ask.com..), do not let webmasters pay to be in their search engine listing (advertisements are shown separately and labeled as such).

Some detractors of paid inclusion allege that it causes searches to return results based more on the economic standing of the interests of a web site, and less on the relevancy of that site to end-users.

Often the line between pay-per-click advertising and paid inclusion is debatable. Some have lobbied for any paid listings to be labeled as an advertisement, while defenders insist they are not actually ads since the webmasters do not control the content of the listing, its ranking, or even whether it is shown to any users. Another advantage of paid inclusion is that it allows site owners to specify particular schedules for crawling pages. In the general case, one has no control as to when their page will be crawled or added to a search engine index. Paid inclusion proves to be particularly useful for cases where pages are dynamically generated and frequently modified.

Paid inclusion is a search engine marketing method in itself, but also a tool of search engine optimization since experts and firms can test out different approaches to improving ranking and see the results often within a couple of days, instead of waiting weeks or months. Knowledge gained this way can be used to optimize other web pages, without paying the search engine company.

5. Comparison with SEO

SEM is the wider discipline that incorporates SEO. SEM includes both paid search results (using tools like Google Adwords or Bing Ads, formerly known as Microsoft adCenter) and organic search results (SEO). SEM uses paid advertising with AdWords or Bing Ads, pay per click (particularly beneficial for local providers as it enables potential consumers to contact a company directly with one click), article submissions, advertising and making sure SEO has been done. A keyword analysis is performed for both SEO and SEM, but not necessarily at the same time. SEM and SEO both need to be monitored and updated frequently to reflect evolving best practices.

In some contexts, the term SEM is used exclusively to mean pay per click advertising,. particularly in the commercial advertising and marketing communities which have a vested interest in this narrow definition. Such usage excludes the wider search marketing community that is engaged in other forms of SEM such as search engine optimization and search retargeting.

Creating the link between SEO and PPC represents an integral part of the SEM concept. Sometimes, especially when separate teams work on SEO and PPC and the efforts are not synced, positive results of aligning their strategies can be lost. The aim of both SEO and PPC is maximizing the visibility in search and thus, their actions to achieve it should be centrally coordinated.Both teams can benefit from setting shared goals and combined metrics, evaluating data together to determine future strategy or discuss which of the tools works better to get the traffic for selected keywords in the national and local search results. Thanks to this, the search visibility can be increased along with optimizing both conversions and costs.

Another part of SEM is social media marketing (SMM). SMM is a type of marketing that involves exploiting social media to influence consumers that one company's products and/or services are valuable. Some of the latest theoretical advances include search engine marketing management (SEMM). SEMM relates to activities including SEO but focuses on return on investment (ROI) management instead of relevant traffic building (as is the case of mainstream SEO). SEMM also integrates organic SEO, trying to achieve top ranking without using paid means to achieve it, and pay-per-click SEO. For example, some of the attention is placed on the web page layout design and how content and information is displayed to the website visitor. SEO & SEM are the two pillars of one marketing job and they both run side by side to produce much better results than focusing on only one pillar.

6. Ethical questions

Paid search advertising has not been without controversy and the issue of how search engines present advertising on their search result pages has been the target of a series of studies and reports by Consumer Reports WebWatch. The Federal Trade Commission (FTC) also issued a letter. in 2002 about the importance of disclosure of paid advertising on search engines, in response to a complaint from Commercial Alert, a consumer advocacy group with ties to Ralph Nader.

Another ethical controversy associated with search marketing has been the issue of trademark infringement. The debate as to whether third parties should have the right to bid on their competitors' brand names has been underway for years. In early 2000 Google changed their policy, which formerly prohibited these tactics, allowing 3rd parties to bid on branded terms as long as their landing page in fact provides information on the trademarked term.. Though the policy has been changed this continues to be a source of heated debate.

On April 24, 2012 up to till date now in 2022, many started to see that Google has started to penalize companies that are buying links for the purpose of passing off the rank. The Google Update was called Penguin. Since then, there have been several different Penguin/Panda updates rolled out by Google. SEM has, however, nothing to do with link buying and focuses on organic SEO and PPC management. As of October 20, 2014 every year till date 2022 and beyond, Google had released three official revisions per year of their Penguin Update.

In 2013, the Tenth Circuit Court of Appeals held in Lens.com, Inc. v. 1-800 Contacts, Inc. that online contact lens seller Lens.com did not commit trademark infringement when it purchased search advertisements using competitor 1-800 Contacts' federally registered 1800 CONTACTS trademark as a keyword. In August 2016, the Federal Trade Commission filed an administrative complaint against 1-800 Contacts alleging, among other things, that its trademark enforcement practices in the search engine marketing space have unreasonably restrained competition in violation of the FTC Act. 1-800 Contacts has denied all wrongdoing and appeared before an FTC administrative law judge in April 2017.

AdWords is now recognized as a web-based advertising utensil since it adopts keywords that can deliver adverts explicitly to web users looking for information in respect to a certain product or service. It is flexible and provides customizable options like Ad Extensions, access to non-search sites, leveraging the display network to help increase brand awareness. The project hinges on cost per click (CPC) pricing where the maximum cost per day for the campaign can be chosen, thus the payment of the service only applies if the advert has been clicked. SEM companies have embarked on AdWords projects as a way to publicize their SEM and SEO services. One of the most successful approaches to the strategy of this project was to focus on making sure that PPC advertising funds were prudently invested. Moreover, SEM companies have described AdWords as a practical tool for increasing a consumer's investment earnings on Internet advertising. The use of conversion tracking and Google Analytics tools was deemed to be practical for presenting to clients the performance of their canvas from click to conversion. AdWords project has enabled SEM companies to train their clients on the utensil and delivers better performance to the canvass. The assistance of AdWord canvass could contribute to the growth of web traffic for a number of its consumer's websites, by as much as 250% in only nine months.

Another way search engine marketing is managed is by contextual advertising. Here marketers place ads on other sites or portals that carry information relevant to their products so that the ads jump into the circle of vision of browsers who are seeking information from those sites.

A successful SEM plan is the approach to capture the relationships amongst information searchers, businesses, and search engines. Search engines were not important to some industries in the past, but over the past years the use of search engines for accessing information has become vital to increase business opportunities. The use of SEM strategic tools for businesses such as tourism can attract potential consumers to view their products, but it could also pose various challenges.. These challenges could be the competition that companies face amongst their industry and other sources of information that could draw the attention of online consumers.. To assist the combat of challenges, the main objective for businesses applying SEM is to improve and maintain their ranking as high as possible on SERPs so that they can gain visibility. Therefore, search engines are adjusting and developing algorithms and the shifting criteria by which web pages are ranked sequentially to combat against search engine misuse and spamming, and to supply the most relevant information to searchers.. This could enhance the relationship amongst information searchers, businesses, and search engines by understanding the strategies of marketing to attract business.

Social media marketing is the use of social media platforms and websites to promote a product or service.. Although the terms e-marketing and digital marketing are still dominant in academia, social media marketing is becoming more popular for both practitioners and researchers. Most social media platforms have built-in data analytics tools, enabling companies to track the progress, success, and engagement of ad campaigns. Companies address a range of stakeholders through social media marketing, including current and potential customers, current and potential employees, journalists, bloggers, and the general public. On a strategic level, social media marketing includes the management of a marketing campaign, governance, setting the scope (e.g. more active or passive use) and the establishment of a firm's desired social media "culture" and "tone."

When using social media marketing, firms can allow the customers and Internet users to post user-generated content (e.g. online comments, product reviews, etc.) also known as "earned media," rather than use marketer-prepared advertising copy.

Platforms - Social media

a) Social networking websites

Social networking websites allow individuals, businesses and other organizations to interact with one another and build relationships and communities online. When companies join these social channels, consumers can interact with them directly. That interaction can be more personal to users than traditional methods of outbound marketing and advertising.

Social networking sites act as a word of mouth or more precisely, e-word of mouth. The Internet's ability to reach billions across the globe has given online word of mouth a powerful voice and far reach. The ability to rapidly change buying patterns, products or service acquisition and activity to a growing number of consumers is defined as influence networks. Social networking sites and blogs allow followers to "retweet" or "repost" comments made by others about a product being promoted, which occurs quite frequently on some social media sites. By repeating the message, the user's connections are able to see the message, therefore reaching more people. Because the information about the product is being put out there and is getting repeated, more traffic is brought to the product/ company.

Social networking websites are based on building virtual communities that allow consumers to express their needs, wants and values, online. Social media marketing then connects these consumers and audiences to businesses that share the same needs, wants, and values. Through social networking sites, companies can keep in touch with individual followers. This personal interaction can instill a feeling of loyalty into followers and potential customers. Also, by choosing whom to follow on these sites, products can reach a very narrow target audience.. Social networking sites also include much information about what products and services prospective clients might be interested in. Through the use of new semantic analysis technologies, marketers can detect buying signals, such as content shared by people and questions posted online. An understanding of buying signals can help sales people target relevant prospects and marketers run micro-targeted campaigns.

In 2014, over 80% of business executives identified social media as an integral part of their business. Business retailers have seen 133% increases in their revenues from social media marketing. Some examples of popular social networking websites over the years are Facebook, Instagram, Twitter, TikTok, MySpace, LinkedIn, and SnapChat.

Mobile phones

Social media apps on a smartphone

More than three billion people in the world are active on the Internet. Over the years, the Internet has continually gained more and more users, jumping from 738 million in 2000 all the way to 3.2 billion in 2015.. Roughly 81% of the current population in the United States has some type of social media profile that they engage with frequently.. Mobile phone usage is beneficial for social media marketing because of their web browsing capabilities which allow individuals immediate access to social networking sites. Mobile phones have altered the path-to-purchase process by allowing consumers to easily obtain pricing and product information in real time. They have also allowed companies to constantly remind and update their followers. Many companies are now putting QR (Quick Response) codes along with products for individuals to access the company website or online services with their smart phones. Retailers use QR codes to facilitate consumer interaction with brands by linking the code to brand websites, promotions, product information, and any other mobile-enabled content. In addition, Real-time bidding use in the mobile advertising industry is high and rising due to its value for on-the-go web browsing. In 2012, Nexage, a provider of real time bidding in mobile advertising reported a 37% increase in revenue each month. Adfonic, another mobile advertisement publishing platform, reported an increase of 22 billion ad requests that same year.

Mobile devices have become increasingly popular, where 5.7 billion people are using them worldwide. This has played a role in the way consumers interact with media and has many further implications for TV ratings, advertising, mobile commerce, and more. Mobile media consumption such as mobile audio streaming or mobile video are on the rise. In the United States, more than 100 million users are projected to access online video content via mobile device. Mobile video revenue consists of pay-per-view downloads, advertising and subscriptions. As of 2013, worldwide mobile phone Internet user penetration was 73.4%. In 2017, figures suggest that more than 90% of Internet users will access online content through their phones.

Strategies

There are the two basic strategies for using social media as a marketing tool:

1. Passive approach

Social media can be a useful source of market information and a way to hear customer perspectives. Blogs, content communities, and forums are platforms where individuals share their reviews and recommendations of brands, products, and services. Businesses are able to tap and analyze the customer voices and feedback generated in social media for marketing purposes;. in this sense the social media is a relatively inexpensive source of market intelligence which can be used by marketers and managers to track and respond to consumer-identified problems and detect market opportunities. For example, the Internet erupted with videos and pictures of iPhone 6 "bend test" which showed that the coveted phone could be bent by hand pressure. The so-called "bend gate" controversy. created confusion amongst customers who had waited months for the launch of the latest rendition of the iPhone. However, Apple promptly issued a statement saying that the problem was extremely rare and that the company had taken several steps to make the mobile device's case stronger and robust. Unlike traditional market research methods such as surveys, focus groups, and data mining which are time-consuming and costly, and which take weeks or even months to analyze, marketers can use social media to obtain 'live' or "real time" information about consumer behavior and viewpoints on a company's brand or products. This can be useful in the highly dynamic, competitive, fast-paced and global marketplace of the 2010s.

2. Active approach

Social media can be used not only as public relations and direct marketing tools, but also as communication channels targeting very specific audiences with social media influencers and social media personalities as effective customer engagement tools.. This tactic is widely known as influencer marketing. Influencer marketing allows brands the opportunity to reach their target audience in a more genuine, authentic way via a special group of selected influencers advertising their product or service. In fact, brands are set to spend up to $15 billion on influencer marketing by 2022, per Business Insider Intelligence estimates, based on Mediakix data.

Technologies predating social media, such as broadcast TV and newspapers can also provide advertisers with a fairly targeted audience, given that an ad placed during a sports game broadcast or in the sports section of a newspaper is likely to be read by sports fans. However, social media websites can target niche markets even more precisely. Using digital tools such as Google AdSense, advertisers can target their ads to very specific demographics, such as people who are interested in social entrepreneurship, political activism associated with a particular political party, or video gaming. Google AdSense does this by looking for keywords in social media user's online posts and comments. It would be hard for a TV station or paper-based newspaper to provide ads that are this targeted (though not impossible, as can be seen with "special issue" sections on niche issues, which newspapers can use to sell targeted ads).

Social networks are, in many cases, viewed as a great tool for avoiding costly market research. They are known for providing a short, fast, and direct way to reach an audience through a person who is widely known. For example, an athlete who gets endorsed by a sporting goods company also brings their support base of millions of people who are interested in what they do or how they play and now they want to be a part of this athlete through their endorsements with that particular company. At one point consumers would visit stores to view their products with famous athletes, but now you can view a famous athlete's, such as Cristiano Ronaldo, latest apparel online with the click of a button. He advertises them to you directly through his Twitter, Instagram, and Facebook accounts.

Facebook and LinkedIn are leading social media platforms where users can hyper-target their ads. Hypertargeting not only uses public profile information but also information users submit but hide from others. There are several examples of firms initiating some form of online dialog with the public to foster relations with customers. According to Constantinides, Lorenzo and Gómez Borja (2008) "Business executives like Jonathan Swartz, President and CEO of Sun Microsystems, Steve Jobs CEO of Apple Computers, and McDonald's Vice President Bob Langert post regularly in their CEO blogs, encouraging customers to interact and freely express their feelings, ideas, suggestions, or remarks about their postings, the company or its products". Using customer influencers (for example popular bloggers) can be a very efficient and cost-effective method to launch new products or services. Among the political leaders in office, Prime Minister Narendra Modi has the highest number of followers at 40M, and President Donald Trump ranks second with 25M followers. Modi employed social media platforms to circumvent traditional media channels to reach out to the young and urban population of India which is estimated to be 200M.

Algorithms

Social media content that has been driven by algorithms has become an increasingly popular feature in the recent years. One social media platform that has used this ground-changing strategy is TikTok. TikTok has become one of the fastest growing applications to date and currently has around 1.5 billion users, mainly consisting of children and teenagers.The algorithm used within this platform encourages creativity among TikTok users because of the platform's wide range of effects and challenges that change from day to day. Because of this feature, content creators big or small have increased chances of going viral by appearing on TikTok's "for you" page. The "for you" page algorithm allows users to have videos recommended to them based on their previous watches, likes and shares.

This can be extremely beneficial for small businesses who are using this platform as a means of social media marketing. Although they may be starting off small, by following trends, using hashtags, & much more, anyone can promote themselves on this emerging application to attract new audiences from all around the world. Moreover, using algorithmically-driven content within TikTok allows for a more positive response rate from users as the target audience tends to be young users, who are more susceptible to these increasingly popular marketing communications.. With this in mind, TikTok is filled with rich content that include images and videos which can beneficially aid influencer marketing over platforms that are heavily text-based as they are less engaging for their audiences.

When considering algorithms in respect to social media platforms, it is evident they can heavily impact the outcomes of this marketing strategy. Since it is a new content feature, younger audiences may respond more positively to it than others, but it is not something that should be disregarded for other audiences. Anyone is able to use this marketing strategy to get themselves out there and engage with new customers or users because of the effective algorithm technique.

Engagement

Engagement with the social web means that customers and stakeholders are active participants rather than passive viewers. An example of these are consumer advocacy groups and groups that criticize companies (e.g., lobby groups or advocacy organizations). Social media use in a business or political context allows all consumers/citizens to express and share an opinion about a company's products, services, business practices, or a government's actions. Each participating customer, non-customer, or citizen who is participating online via social media becomes a part of the marketing department (or a challenge to the marketing effort) as other customers read their positive or negative comments or reviews. Getting consumers, potential consumers or citizens to be engaged online is fundamental to successful social media marketing.. With the advent of social media marketing, it has become increasingly important to gain customer interest in products and services. This can eventually be translated into buying behavior, or voting and donating behavior in a political context. New online marketing concepts of engagement and loyalty have emerged which aim to build customer participation and brand reputation.

Engagement in social media for the purpose of a social media strategy is divided into two parts. Thc first is proactive, regular posting of new online content. This can be seen through digital photos, digital videos, text, and conversations It is also represented through sharing of content & information from others via weblinks. The second part is reactive conversations with social media users responding to those who reach out to your social media profiles through commenting or messaging. Traditional media such as TV news shows are limited to one-way interaction with customers or 'push and tell' where only specific information is given to the customer with few or limited mechanisms to obtain customer feedback. Traditional media such as physical newspapers, do give readers the option of sending a letter to the editor. Though, this is a relatively slow process, as the editorial board has to review the letter and decide if it is appropriate for publication. On the other hand, social media is participative and open; Participants are able to instantly share their views on brands, products, and services. Traditional media gave control of message to the marketer, whereas social media shifts the balance to the consumer or citizen.

Campaigns

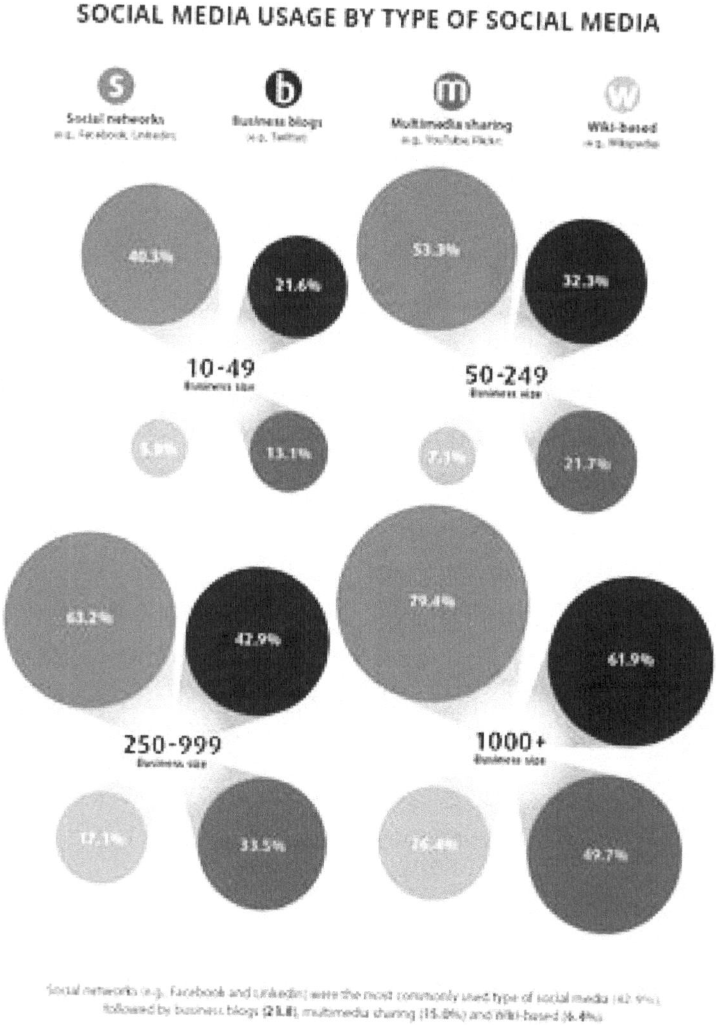

Business use of social media in the UK

Local businesses

Small businesses also use social networking sites as a promotional technique. Businesses can follow individuals' social networking site uses in the local area and advertise specials and deals. These can be exclusive and in the form of "get a free drink with a copy of this tweet". This type of message encourages other locals to follow the business on the sites in order to obtain the promotional deal. In the process, the business is getting seen and promoting itself (brand visibility).

Small businesses also use social networking sites to develop their own market research on new products and services. By encouraging their customers to give feedback on new product ideas, businesses can gain valuable insights on whether a product may be accepted by their target market enough to merit full production, or not. In addition, customers will feel the company has engaged them in the process of co-creation—the process in which the business uses customer feedback to create or modify a product or service, filling a need of the target market. Such feedback can be presented in various forms, such as surveys, contests, polls, etc.

Social networking sites such as LinkedIn, also provide an opportunity for small businesses to find candidates to fill staff positions.

Of course, review sites, such as Yelp, also help small businesses to build their reputation beyond just brand visibility. Positive customer peer reviews help to influence new prospects to purchase goods and services more than company advertising.

Nike #MakeItCount

In early 2022, Nike introduced its Make It Count social media campaign. The campaign kickoff began with YouTubers Casey Neistat and Max Joseph launching a YouTube video, where they traveled 34,000 miles to visit 16 cities in 13 countries. They promoted the #makeitcount hashtag, which millions of consumers shared via Twitter and Instagram by uploading photos and sending tweets. The #TheMakeItCount YouTube video went viral and Nike saw an 18% increase in profit in 2022, the year this product was released.

Purposes and tactics

One of the main purposes of employing social media in marketing is as a communications tool that makes the companies accessible to those interested in their product and makes them visible to those who have no knowledge of their products. These companies use social media to create buzz, and learn from and target customers. It's the only form of marketing that can finger consumers at each and every stage of the consumer decision journey. Marketing through social media has other benefits as well. Of the top 10 factors that correlate with a strong Google organic search, seven are social media dependent. This means that if brands are less or non-active on social media, they tend to show up less on Google searches. While platforms such as Twitter, Facebook and Google+ have a larger number of monthly users, the visual media sharing based mobile platforms however, garner a higher interaction rate in comparison and have registered the fastest growth and have changed the ways in which consumers engage with brand content. Instagram has an interaction rate of 1.46% with an average of

130M users monthly as opposed to Twitter which has a 0.03% interaction rate with an average of 210M monthly users. Unlike traditional media that are often cost-prohibitive to many companies, a social media strategy does not require astronomical budgeting.

To this end, companies make use of platforms such as Facebook, Twitter, YouTube, TikTok and Instagram to reach audiences much wider than through the use of traditional print/TV/radio advertisements alone at a fraction of the cost, as most social networking sites can be used at little or no cost (however, some websites charge companies for premium services). This has changed the ways that companies approach to interact with customers, as a substantial percentage of consumer interactions are now being carried out over online platforms with much higher visibility. Customers can now post reviews of products and services, rate customer service, and ask questions or voice concerns directly to companies through social media platforms. According to Measuring Success, over 80% of consumers use the web to research products and services. Thus, social media marketing is also used by businesses in order to build relationships of trust with consumers. To this aim, companies may also hire personnel to specifically handle these social media interactions, who usually report under the title online community managers. Handling these interactions in a satisfactory manner can result in an increase of consumer trust. To both this aim and to fix the public's perception of a company, 3 steps are taken in order to address consumer concerns, identifying the extent of the social chatter, engaging the influencers to help, and developing a proportional response.

Twitter

Twitter allows companies to promote their products in short messages known as tweets limited to 280 characters which appear on followers' Home timelines.. Tweets can contain text, Hashtag, photo, video, Animated GIF, Emoji, or links to the product's website and other social media profiles, etc.. Twitter is also used by companies to provide customer service.. Some companies make support available 24/7 and answer promptly, thus improving brand loyalty and appreciation.

Facebook

Facebook pages are far more detailed than Twitter accounts. They allow a product to provide videos, photos, longer descriptions, and testimonials where followers can comment on the product pages for others to see. Facebook can link back to the product's Twitter page, as well as send out event reminders. As of May 2015, 93% of businesses marketers use Facebook to promote their brand. A study from 2021 attributed 84% of "engagement" or clicks and likes that link back to Facebook advertising. By 2022, Facebook had restricted the content published from business and brand pages. Adjustments in Facebook algorithms have reduced the audience for non-paying business pages (that have at least 500,000 "Likes") from 16% in 2012 down to 2% in February 2022.

LinkedIn

LinkedIn, a professional business-related networking site, allows companies to create professional profiles for themselves as well as their business to network and meet others. Through the use of widgets, members can promote their various social networking activities, such as Twitter streams or blog entries of their product pages, onto their LinkedIn profile page. LinkedIn provides its members opportunity to generate sales leads and business partners. Members can use "Company Pages" similar to Facebook pages to create an area that will allow business owners to promote their products or services and be able to interact with their customers.

Whatsapp

WhatsApp was founded by Jan Koum and Brian Acton.

Joining Facebook in 2014, WhatsApp continues to operate as a separate app with a laser focus on building a messaging service that works fast and reliably anywhere in the world. Started as an alternative to SMS, WhatsApp now supports sending and receiving a variety of media including text, photos, videos, documents, and location, as well as voice calls. WhatsApp messages and calls are secured with end-to-end encryption, meaning that no third party including WhatsApp can read or listen to them. WhatsApp has a customer base of 1 billion people in over 180 countries. It is used to send personalized promotional messages to individual customers. It has plenty of advantages over SMS that includes the ability to track how Message Broadcast Performs using the blue tick option in WhatsApp. It allows sending messages to Do Not Disturb (DND) customers. WhatsApp is also used to send a series of bulk messages to their targeted customers using the broadcast option. Companies started using this to a large extent because it is a cost-effective promotional option and quick to spread a message. As of 2019, WhatsApp still does not allow businesses to place ads in their app.

Yelp

Yelp consists of a comprehensive online index of business profiles. Businesses are searchable by location, similar to Yellow Pages. The website is operational in seven different countries, including the United States and Canada. Business account holders are allowed to create, share, and edit business profiles. They may post information such as business location, contact information, pictures, and service information. The website further allows individuals to write, post reviews about businesses, and rate them on a five-point scale. Messaging and talk features are further made available for general members of the website, serving to guide thoughts and opinions.

Instagram

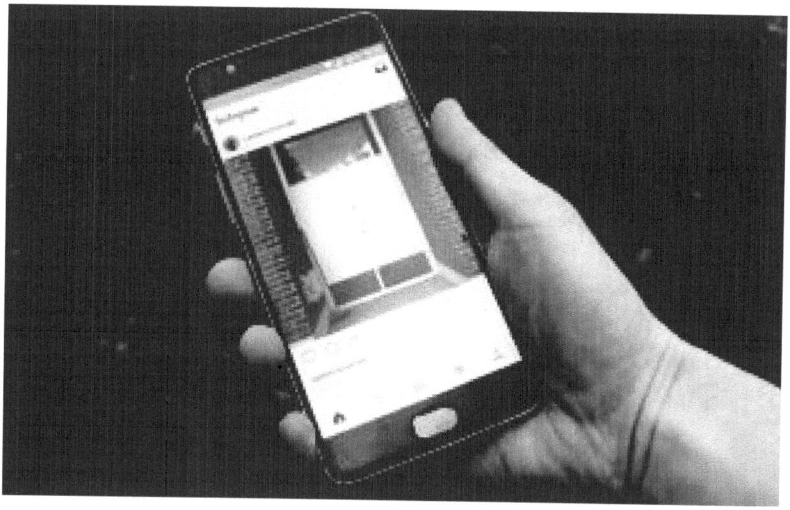

The Instagram app

In May 2014, Instagram had over 200M users. The user engagement rate of Instagram was 15 times higher than of Facebook and 25 times higher than that of Twitter. According to Scott Galloway, the founder of L2 and a professor of Marketing at New York University's Stern School of Business, latest studies estimate that 93% of prestige brands have an active presence on Instagram and include it in their marketing mix. When it comes to brands and businesses, Instagram's goal is to help companies to reach their respective audiences through captivating imagery in a rich, visual environment. Moreover, Instagram provides a platform where users and companies can communicate publicly and directly, making itself an ideal platform for companies to connect with their current and potential customers.

Many brands are now heavily using this mobile app to boost their marketing strategy. Instagram can be used to gain the necessary momentum needed to capture the attention of the market segment that has an interest in the product offering or services. As Instagram is supported by both Apple and Android systems, it can be easily accessed by smartphone users. Moreover, it can be accessed by the Internet as well. Thus, the marketers see it as a potential platform to expand their brands exposure to the public, especially the younger target group. On top of this, the marketers do not only use the social media for traditional Internet advertising, but they also encourage users to create attention for a certain brand. This generally creates an opportunity for greater brand exposure. Furthermore,marketers are also using the platform to drive social shopping and inspire people to collect and share pictures of their favorite products. Many big names have already jumped on board: Starbucks, MTV, Nike, Marc Jacobs, and Red Bull are a few examples of multinationals that adopted the mobile photo app early. Fashion blogger Danielle Bernstein, who goes by @weworewhat on Instagram, collaborated with Harper's Bazaar to do a piece on how brands are using Instagram to market their products, and how bloggers make money from it. Bernstein, who currently has one and a half million followers on Instagram, and whose "outfit of the day" photos on Snapchat get tens of thousands of screenshots, explained that for a lot of her sponsored posts, she must feature the brand in a certain number of posts, and often cannot wear a competitor's product in the same picture. According to Harper's Bazaar, industry estimates say that brands are spending more than $1 billion per year on consumer-generated advertising.

Instagram has proven itself a powerful platform for marketers to reach their customers and prospects through sharing pictures and brief messages. According to a study by Simply Measured, 71% of the world's largest brands are now using Instagram as a marketing channel.. For companies, Instagram can be used as a tool to connect and communicate with current and potential customers. The company can present a more personal picture of their brand, and by doing so the company conveys a better and true picture of itself. The idea of Instagram pictures lies on-the-go, a sense that the event is happening right now, and that adds another layer to the personal and accurate picture of the company. In fact, Thomas Rankin, co-founder and CEO of the program Dash Hudson, stated that when he approves a blogger's Instagram post before it is posted on the behalf of a brand his company represents, his only negative feedback is if it looks too posed. "It's not an editorial photo," he explained, "We're not trying to be a magazine. We're trying to create a moment."

Another option Instagram provides the opportunity for companies to reflect a true picture of the brand from the perspective of the customers, for instance, using the user-generated contents thought the hashtags encouragement. Other than the filters and hashtags functions, the Instagram's 15-second videos and the recently added ability to send private messages between users have opened new opportunities for brands to connect with customers in a new extent, further promoting effective marketing on Instagram.

Snapchat

Snapchat is a popular messaging and picture exchanging application that was created in 2011 by three students at Stanford University named Evan Spiegel, Bobby Murphy, and Reggie Brown. The application was first developed to allow users to message back and forth and to also send photographs that are only available from 1–10 seconds until they are no longer available. The app was an instant hit with social media members and today there are up to 158 million people using snapchat every single day. It is also estimated that Snapchat users are opening the application approximately 18 times per day, which means users are on the app for about 25–30 minutes per day.

YouTube

YouTube is another popular avenue; advertisements are done in a way to suit the target audience. The type of language used in the commercials and the ideas used to promote the product reflect the audience's style and taste. Also, the ads on this platform are usually in sync with the content of the video requested, this is another advantage YouTube brings for advertisers. Certain ads are presented with certain videos since the content is relevant. Promotional opportunities such as sponsoring a video is also possible on YouTube, "for example, a user who searches for a YouTube video on dog training may be presented with a sponsored video from a dog toy company in results along with other videos.". YouTube also enable publishers to earn money through its YouTube Partner Program. Companies can pay YouTube for a special "channel" which promotes the companies products or services.

Social bookmarking sites

Websites such as Delicious, Digg, Slashdot, Diigo, Stumbleupon, and Reddit are popular social bookmarking sites used in social media promotion. Each of these sites is dedicated to the collection, curation, and organization of links to other websites that users deem to be of good quality. This process is "crowdsourced", allowing amateur social media network members to sort and prioritize links by relevance and general category. Due to the large user bases of these websites, any link from one of them to another, the smaller website may in a flash crowd, a sudden surge of interest in the target website. In addition to user-generated promotion, these sites also offer advertisements within individual user communities and categories. Because ads can be placed in designated communities with a very specific target audience and demographic, they have far greater potential for traffic generation than ads selected simply through cookie and browser history.. Additionally, some of these websites have also implemented measures to make ads more relevant to users by allowing users to vote on which ones will be shown on pages they frequent. The ability to redirect large volumes of web traffic and target specific, relevant audiences makes social bookmarking sites a valuable asset for social media marketers.

Blogs

A Wordpress blog

Platforms like LinkedIn create an environment for companies and clients to connect online. Companies that recognize the need for information, originality and accessibility employ blogs to make their products popular and unique/ and ultimately reach out to consumers who are privy to social media.. Studies from 2009 show that consumers view coverage in the media or from bloggers as being more neutral and credible than print advertisements, which are not thought of as free or independent.. Blogs allow a product or company to provide longer descriptions of products or services, can include testimonials and can link to and from other social network and blog pages. Blogs can be updated frequently and are promotional techniques for keeping customers, and also for acquiring followers and subscribers who can then be directed to social network pages. Online communities can enable a business to reach the clients of other businesses using the platform. To allow firms to measure their standing in the corporate world, sites enable employees to place evaluations of their companies.

Some businesses opt out of integrating social media platforms into their traditional marketing regimen. There are also specific corporate standards that apply when interacting online.. To maintain an advantage in a business-consumer relationship, businesses have to be aware of four key assets that consumers maintain: information, involvement, community, and control.

Tumblr

Blogging website Tumblr first launched ad products on May 29, 2012.. Rather than relying on simple banner ads, Tumblr requires advertisers to create a Tumblr blog so the content of those blogs can be featured on the site.. In one year, four native ad formats were created on web and mobile, and had more than 100 brands advertising on Tumblr with 500 cumulative sponsored posts.

Ad formats

- Sponsored mobile post – Advertisements (Advertisers' blog posts) will show up on the user's Dashboard when the user is on a mobile device such as smartphones and tablets, allowing them to like, reblog, and share the sponsored post.

- Sponsored web post – "Largest in-stream ad unit on the web" that catches the users' attention when looking at their Dashboard through their computer or laptop. It also allows the viewers to like, reblog, and share it.

- Sponsored radar – Radar picks up exceptional posts from the whole Tumblr community based on their originality and creativity. It is placed on the right side next to the Dashboard, and it typically earns 120 million daily impressions. Sponsored radar allows advertisers to place their posts there to have an opportunity to earn new followers, reblogs, and likes.

- Sponsored spotlight – Spotlight is a directory of some of the popular blogs throughout the community and a place where users can find new blogs to follow. Advertisers can choose one category out of fifty categories that they can have their blog listed on there.

These posts can be one or more of the following: images, photo sets, animated GIFs, video, audio, and text posts. For the users to differentiate the promoted posts to the regular users' posts, the promoted posts have a dollar symbol on the corner. On May 6, 2014, Tumblr announced customization and theming on mobile apps for brands to advertise.

Advertising campaigns

- Disney/Pixar's Monsters University: Created a Tumblr account, MUGrumblr, saying that the account is maintained by a 'Monstropolis transplant' and 'self-diagnosed coffee addict' who is currently a sophomore at Monsters University.A "student" from Monsters University uploaded memes, animated GIFs, and Instagram-like photos that are related to the sequel movie.

- Apple's iPhone 5c: Created a Tumblr page, labeling it "Every color has a story" with the website name: "ISee5c". As soon as you visit the website, the page is covered with different colors representing the iPhone 5c phone colors and case colors. When you click on one of the colored section, a 15-second video plays a song and "showcases the dots featured on the rear of the iPhone 5c official cases and on the iOS 7 dynamic wallpapers." concluding with words that are related to the video's theme.

Marketing techniques

Social media marketing involves the use of social networks, consumer's online brand-related activities (COBRA) and electronic word of mouth (eWOM). to successfully advertise online. Social networks such as Facebook and Twitter provide advertisers with information about the likes and dislikes of their consumers.. This technique is crucial, as it provides the businesses with a "target audience". With social networks, information relevant to the user's likes is available to businesses; who then advertise accordingly. Activities such as uploading a picture of your "new Converse sneakers to Facebook." is an example of a COBRA. Electronic recommendations and appraisals are a convenient manner to have a product promoted via "consumer-to-consumer interactions.. An example of eWOM would be an online hotel review;. the hotel company can have two possible outcomes based on their service. A good service would result in a positive review which gets the hotel free advertising via social media. However, a poor service will result in a negative consumer review which can potentially harm the company's reputation.

Social networking sites such as Facebook, Instagram, Twitter, MySpace etc. have all influenced the buzz of word of mouth marketing. In 1999, Misner said that word-of mouth marketing is, "the world's most effective, yet least understood marketing strategy" (Trusov, Bucklin, & Pauwels, 2009, p. 3). Through the influence of opinion leaders, the increased online "buzz" of "word-of-mouth" marketing that a product, service or companies are experiencing is due to the rise in use of social media and smartphones. Businesses and marketers have noticed that, "a person's behaviour is influenced by many small groups" (Kotler, Burton, Deans, Brown, & Armstrong, 2013, p. 189). These small groups rotate around social networking accounts that are run by influential people (opinion leaders or "thought leaders") who have followers of groups. The types of groups (followers) are called:. reference groups (people who know each other either face-to-face or have an indirect influence on a persons attitude or behaviour); membership groups (a person has a direct influence on a person's attitude or behaviour); and aspirational groups (groups which an individual wishes to belong to).

Influencer marketing

Chiara Ferragni is a fashion influencer and blogger known for her sponsored fashion posts.

Marketers target influential people, referred to as influencers, on social media who are recognized as being opinion leaders and opinion-formers to send messages to their target audiences and amplify the impact of their message. A social media post by an opinion leader can have a much greater impact (via the forwarding of the post or "liking" of the post) than a social media post by a regular user. Marketers have come to the understanding that "consumers are more prone to believe in other individuals" who they trust (Sepp, Liljander, & Gummerus, 2011). OL's and OF's can also send their own messages about products and services they choose (Fill, Hughes, & De Francesco, 2013, p. 216). The reason the opinion leader or formers have such a strong following base is because their opinion is valued or trusted (Clement, Proppe, & Rott, 2007). They can review products and services for their followings, which can be positive or negative towards the brand. OL's and OF's are people who have a social status and because of their personality, beliefs, values etc. have the potential to influence other people (Kotler, Burton, Deans, Brown, & Armstrong, 2013, p. 189). They usually have a large number of followers otherwise known as their reference, membership or aspirational group (Kotler, Burton, Deans, Brown, & Armstrong), 2013, p. 189. By having an OL or OF support a brands product by posting a photo, video or written recommendation on a blog, the following may be influenced and because they trust the OL/OF a high chance of the brand selling more products or creating a following base. Having an OL/OF helps spread word of mouth talk amongst reference groups and/or memberships groups e.g. family, friends, work-friends etc. (Kotler, Burton, Deans, Brown, & Armstrong, 2013, p. 189). The adjusted communication model shows the use of using opinion leaders and opinion formers. The sender/source gives the message to many, many OL's/OF's who pass the message on along with their personal opinion, the receiver (followers/groups) form their own opinion and send their personal message to their group (friends, family etc.) (Dahlen, Lange, & Smith, 2010, p. 39).

Organic Social Media

Owned social media channels are an essential extension of business' and brands in today's world. Brand must seek to create their brand image on each platform, and cater to the type of consumer demographics on each respective platform. In contrast with pre-Internet marketing, such as TV ads and newspaper ads, in which the marketer controlled all aspects of the ad, with social media, users are free to post comments right below an online ad or an online post by a company about its product. Companies are increasing using their social media strategy as part of their traditional marketing effort using magazines, newspapers, radio advertisements, television advertisements. Since in the 2010s, media consumers are often using multiple platforms at the same time (e.g., surfing the Internet on a tablet while watching a streaming TV show), marketing content needs to be consistent across all platforms, whether traditional or new media. Heath (2006) wrote about the extent of attention businesses should give to their social media sites. It is about finding a balance between frequently posting but not over posting. There is a lot more attention to be paid towards social media sites because people need updates to gain brand recognition. Therefore, a lot more content is need and this can often be unplanned content.

Planned content begins with the creative/marketing team generating their ideas, once they have completed their ideas they send them off for approval. There is two general ways of doing so. The first is where each sector approves the plan one after another, editor, brand, followed by the legal team (Brito, 2013). Sectors may differ depending on the size and philosophy of the business. The second is where each sector is given 24 hours (or such designated time) to sign off or disapprove. If no action is given within the 24-hour period the original plan is implemented. Planned content is often noticeable to customers and is un-original or lacks excitement but is also a safer option to avoid unnecessary backlash from the public.. Both routes for planned content are time-consuming as in the above; the first way to approval takes 72 hours to be approved. Although the second route can be significantly shorter it also holds more risk particularly in the legal department.

Unplanned content is an 'in the moment' idea, "a spontaneous, tactical reaction." (Cramer, 2014, p. 6). The content could be trending and not have the time to take the planned content route. The unplanned content is posted sporadically and is not calendar/date/time arranged (Deshpande, 2014)... Issues with unplanned content revolve around legal issues and whether the message being sent out represents the business/brand accordingly. If a company sends out a Tweet or Facebook message too hurriedly, the company may unintentionally use insensitive language or messaging that could alienate some consumers. For example, celebrity chef Paula Deen was criticized after she made a social media post commenting about HIV-AIDS and South Africa; her message was deemed to be offensive by many observers. The main difference between planned and unplanned is the time to approve the content. Unplanned content must still be approved by marketing managers, but in a much more rapid manner e.g. 1–2 hours or less. Sectors may miss errors because of being hurried. When using unplanned content Brito (2013) says, "be prepared to be reactive and respond to issues when they arise.". Brito (2013) writes about having a, "crisis escalation plan", because, "It will happen". The plan involves breaking down the issue into topics and classifying the issue into groups. Colour coding the potential risk "identify and flag potential risks" also helps to organise an issue. The problem can then be handled by the correct team and dissolved more effectively rather than any person at hand trying to solve the situation.

Implications on traditional advertising

Minimizing use

Traditional advertising techniques include print and television advertising. The Internet has already overtaken television as the largest advertising market.. Web sites often include the banner or pop-up ads. Social networking sites don't always have ads. In exchange, products have entire pages and are able to interact with users. Television commercials often end with a spokesperson asking viewers to check out the product website for more information. While briefly popular, print ads included QR codes on them. These QR codes can be scanned by cell phones and computers, sending viewers to the product website. Advertising is beginning to move viewers from the traditional outlets to the electronic ones.. While traditional media, like newspapers and television advertising, are largely overshadowed by the rise of social media marketing, there is still a place for traditional marketing. For example, with newspapers, readership over the years has shown a decline. However, readership with newspapers is still fiercely loyal to print-only media. 51% of newspaper readers only read the newspaper in its print form,. making well-placed ads valuable.

Leaks

The Internet and social networking leaks are one of the issues facing traditional advertising. Video and print ads are often leaked to the world via the Internet earlier than they are scheduled to premiere. Social networking sites allow those leaks to go viral, and be seen by many users more quickly. The time difference is also a problem facing traditional advertisers. When social events occur and are broadcast on television, there is often a time delay between airings on the east coast and west coast of the United States. Social networking sites have become a hub of comment and interaction concerning the event. This allows individuals watching the event on the west coast (time-delayed) to know the outcome before it airs. The 2011 Grammy Awards highlighted this problem. Viewers on the west coast learned who won different awards based on comments made on social networking sites by individuals watching live on the east coast.. Since viewers knew who won already, many tuned out and ratings were lower. All the advertisement and promotion put into the event was lost because viewers didn't have a reason to watch.[according to whom?]

Mishaps

Social media marketing provides organizations with a way to connect with their customers. However, organizations must protect their information as well as closely watch comments and concerns on the social media they use. A flash poll done on 1225 IT executives from 33 countries revealed that social media mishaps caused organizations a combined $4.3 million in damages in 2010.. The top three social media incidents an organization faced during the previous year included employees sharing too much information in public forums, loss or exposure of confidential information, and increased exposure to litigation.. Due to the viral nature of the Internet, a mistake by a single employee has in some cases shown to result in devastating consequences for organizations. An example of a social media mishap includes designer Kenneth Cole's Twitter mishap in 2011. When Kenneth Cole tweeted, "Millions are in uproar in #Cairo. Rumor has they heard our new spring collection is now available online at .". This reference to the 2011 Egyptian revolution drew an objection from the public; it was widely objected to on the Internet.Kenneth Cole realized his mistake shortly after and responded with a statement apologizing for the tweet.

In 2012 during Hurricane Sandy, Gap sent out a tweet to its followers telling them to stay safe but encouraged them to shop online and offered free shipping. The tweet was deemed insensitive, and Gap eventually took it down and apologized. Numerous additional online marketing mishap examples exist. Examples include a YouTube video of a Domino's Pizza employee violating health code standards, which went viral on the Internet and later resulted in felony charges against two employees. A Twitter hashtag posted by McDonald's in 2012 attracting attention due to numerous complaints and negative events customers experienced at the chain store; and a 2011 tweet posted by a Chrysler Group employee that no one in Detroit knows how to drive.. When the Link REIT opened a Facebook page to recommend old-style restaurants, the page was flooded by furious comments criticizing the REIT for having forced a lot of restaurants and stores to shut down; it had to terminate its campaign early amid further deterioration of its corporate image.

In 2018, Max Factor, MAC and other beauty brands were forced to rush to disassociate themselves from Kuwaiti beauty blogger and Instagram 'influencer' Sondos Alqattan after she criticised government moves to improve conditions for domestic workers.

Ethics

The code of ethics that is affiliated with traditional marketing can also be applied to social media.. However, with social media being so personal and international, there is another list of complications and challenges that come along with being ethical online. A sensitive topic about social media professionals is the subject of ethics in social media marketing practices, specifically: the proper uses of, often, very personal data.. With the invention of social media, the marketer no longer has to focus solely on the basic demographics and psychographics given from television and magazines, but now they can see what consumers like to hear from advertisers, how they engage online, and what their needs and wants are. The general concept of being ethical while marking on social network sites is to be honest with the intentions of the campaign, avoid false advertising, be aware of user privacy conditions (which means not using consumers' private information for gain), respect the dignity of persons in the shared online community, and claim responsibility for any mistakes or mishaps that are results of your marketing campaign.. Most social network marketers use websites like Facebook andMySpace to try to drive traffic to another website.. While it is ethical to use social networking websites to spread a message to people who are genuinely interested, many people game the system with auto-friend adding programs and spam messages and bulletins. Social networking websites are becoming wise to these practices, however, and are effectively weeding out and banning offenders.

In addition, social media platforms have become extremely aware of their users and collect information about their viewers to connect with them in various ways. Social-networking website Facebook Inc. is quietly working on a new advertising system that would let marketers target users with ads based on the massive amounts of information people reveal on the site about themselves.. This may be an unethical or ethical feature to some individuals. Some people may react negatively because they believe it is an invasion of privacy. On the other hand, some individuals may enjoy this feature because their social network recognizes their interests and sends them particular advertisements pertaining to those interests. Consumers like to network with people who share their interests and desires. Individuals who agree to have their social media profile public, should be aware that advertisers have the ability to take information that interests them to be able to send them information and advertisements to boost their sales. Managers invest in social media to foster relationships and interact with customers.. This is an ethical way for managers to send messages about their advertisements and products to their consumers.

Since social media marketing first came into being, strategists and marketers have been getting smarter and more careful with the way they collect information and distributing advertisements. With the presence of data collecting companies, there is no longer a need to target specific audiences. This can be seen as a large ethically gray area. For many users, this is a breach of privacy, but there are no laws that prevent these companies from using the information provided on their websites. Companies like Equifax, Inc., TransUnion Corp, and LexisNexis Group thrive on collecting and sharing personal information of social media users.. In 2012, Facebook purchased information from 70 million households from a third party company called Datalogix. Facebook later revealed that they purchased the information in order to create a more efficient advertising service.

Facebook had an estimated 144.27 million views in 2016, approximately 12.9 million per month.. Despite this high volume of traffic, very little has been done to protect the millions of users who log on to Facebook and other social media platforms each month. President Barack Obama tried to work with the Federal Trade Commission (FTC) to attempt to regulate data mining. He proposed the Privacy Bill of Rights, which would protect the average user from having their private information downloaded and shared with third party companies. The proposed laws would give the consumer more control over what information companies can collect. President Obama was unable to pass most of these laws through congress, and it is unsure what President Trump will do with regards to social media marketing ethics.

Web development is the work involved in developing a website for the Internet (World Wide Web) or an intranet (a private network). Web development can range from developing a simple single static page of plain text to complex web applications, electronic businesses, and social network services. A more comprehensive list of tasks to which Web development commonly refers, may include Web engineering, Web design, Web content development, client liaison, client-side/server-side scripting, Web server and network security configuration, and e-commerce development.

Among Web professionals, "Web development" usually refers to the main non-design aspects of building Web sites: writing markup and coding. Web development may use content management systems (CMS) to make content changes easier and available with basic technical skills.

For larger organizations and businesses, Web development teams can consist of hundreds of people (Web developers) and follow standard methods like Agile methodologies while developing Web sites. Smaller organizations may only require a single permanent or contracting developer, or secondary assignment to related job positions such as a graphic designer or information systems technician. Web development may be a collaborative effort between departments rather than the domain of a designated department. There are three kinds of Web developer specialization: front-end developer, back-end developer, and full-stack developer.. Front-end developers are responsible for behavior and visuals that run in the user browser, while back-end developers deal with the servers. Since the commercialization of the Web with Tim Berners-Lee.

developing the World Wide Web at CERN, the industry has boomed and has become one of the most used technologies ever.

Web design encompasses many different skills and disciplines in the production and maintenance of websites. The different areas of web design include web graphic design; user interface design (UI design); authoring, including standardised code and proprietary software; user experience design (UX design); and search engine optimization. Often many individuals will work in teams covering different aspects of the design process, although some designers will cover them all. The term "web design" is normally used to describe the design process relating to the front-end (client side) design of a website including writing markup. Web design partially overlaps web engineering in the broader scope of web development. Web designers are expected to have an awareness of usability and be up to date with web accessibility guidelines.

History

Web design books in a store

1988–2001

Although web design has a fairly recent history, it can be linked to other areas such as graphic design, user experience, and multimedia arts, but is more aptly seen from a technological standpoint. It has become a large part of people's everyday lives. It is hard to imagine the Internet without animated graphics, different styles of typography, background, videos and music.

The start of the web and Web design

In 1989, whilst working at CERN Tim Berners-Lee proposed to create a global hypertext project, which later became known as the World Wide Web. During 1991 to 1993 the World Wide Web was born. Text-only HTML pages could be viewed using a simple line-mode web browser. In 1993 Marc Andreessen and Eric Bina, created the Mosaic browser. At the time there were multiple browsers, however the majority of them were Unix-based and naturally text heavy. There had been no integrated approach to graphic design elements such as images or sounds. The Mosaic browser broke this mould. The W3C was created in October 1994 to "lead the World Wide Web to its full potential by developing common protocols that promote its evolution and ensure its interoperability.". This discouraged any one company from monopolizing a propriety browser and programming language, which could have altered the effect of the World Wide Web as a whole. The W3C continues to set standards, which can today be seen with JavaScript and other languages. In 1994 Andreessen formed Mosaic Communications Corp. that later became known as Netscape Communications, the Netscape 0.9 browser. Netscape created its own HTML tags without regard to the traditional standards process. For example, Netscape 1.1 included tags for changing background colours and formatting text with tables on web pages. Throughout 1996 to 1999 the browser wars began, as Microsoft and Netscape fought for ultimate browser dominance. During this time there were many new technologies in the field, notably Cascading Style Sheets, JavaScript, and Dynamic HTML. On the whole, the browser competition did lead to many positive creations and helped web design evolve at a rapid pace.

Evolution of Web Design

In 1996, Microsoft released its first competitive browser, which was complete with its own features and HTML tags. It was also the first browser to support style sheets, which at the time was seen as an obscure authoring technique and is today an important aspect of web design.. The HTML markup for tables was originally intended for displaying tabular data.

However designers quickly realized the potential of using HTML tables for creating the complex, multi-column layouts that were otherwise not possible. At this time, as design and good aesthetics seemed to take precedence over good mark-up structure, and little attention was paid to semantics and web accessibility. HTML sites were limited in their design options, even more so with earlier versions of HTML. To create complex designs, many web designers had to use complicated table structures or even use blank spacer .GIF images to stop empty table cells from collapsing.. CSS was introduced in December 1996 by the W3C to support presentation and layout. This allowed HTML code to be semantic rather than both semantic and presentational, and improved web accessibility, see tableless web design.

In 1996, Flash (originally known as FutureSplash) was developed. At the time, the Flash content development tool was relatively simple compared to now, using basic layout and drawing tools, a limited precursor to ActionScript, and a timeline, but it enabled web designers to go beyond the point of HTML, animated GIFs and JavaScript. However, because Flash required a plug-in, many web developers avoided using it for fear of limiting their market share due to lack of compatibility. Instead, designers reverted to gif animations (if they didn't forego using motion graphics altogether) and JavaScript for widgets. But the benefits of Flash made it popular enough among specific target markets to eventually work its way to the vast majority of browsers, and powerful enough to be used to develop entire sites.

End of the first browser wars

In 1998, Netscape released Netscape Communicator code under an open source licence, enabling thousands of developers to participate in improving the software. However, these developers decided to start a standard for the web from scratch, which guided the development of the open source browser and soon expanded to a complete application platform.. The Web Standards Project was formed and promoted browser compliance with HTML and CSS standards. Programs like Acid1, Acid2, and Acid3 were created in order to test browsers for compliance with web standards. In 2000, Internet Explorer was released for Mac, which was the first browser that fully supported HTML 4.01 and CSS 1. It was also the first browser to fully support the PNG image format.. By 2001, after a campaign by Microsoft to popularize Internet Explorer, Internet Explorer had reached 96% of web browser usage share, which signified the end of the first browsers wars as Internet Explorer had no real competition.

2001–2021

Since the start of the 21st century the web has become more and more integrated into peoples lives. As this has happened the technology of the web has also moved on. There have also been significant changes in the way people use and access the web, and this has changed how sites are designed.

Since the end of the browsers wars new browsers have been released. Many of these are open source meaning that they tend to have faster development and are more supportive of new standards. The new options are considered by many[weasel words] to be better than Microsoft's Internet Explorer.

The W3C has released new standards for HTML (HTML5) and CSS (CSS3), as well as new JavaScript API's, each as a new but individual standard.[when?] While the term HTML5 is only used to refer to the new version of HTML and some of the JavaScript API's, it has become common to use it to refer to the entire suite of new standards (HTML5, CSS3 and JavaScript).

2012 -2023

With the improvement of 3G and LTE internet coverage, large part of website traffic became mobile-generated. This affected the web design industry, pushing it towards minimalistic, lightened and simplistic style. In particular, the "Mobile first" approach emerged, which implies creating website design with mobile-oriented layout first, and then adapting it to higher screen dimensions.

Tools and technologies

Web designers use a variety of different tools depending on what part of the production process they are involved in. These tools are updated over time by newer standards and software but the principles behind them remain the same. Web designers use both vector and raster graphics editors to create web-formatted imagery or design prototypes. A website can be created using WYSIWYG website builder software or content management system, or the individual web pages can be hand-coded in just the same manner as the first web pages were created. Other tools web designers might use include mark up validators. and other testing tools for usability and accessibility to ensure their websites meet web accessibility guidelines.

Skills and techniques

1. Marketing and communication design

Marketing and communication design on a website may identify what works for its target market. This can be an age group or particular strand of culture; thus the designer may understand the trends of its audience. Designers may also understand the type of website they are designing, meaning, for example, that (B2B) business-to-business website design considerations might differ greatly from a consumer targeted website such as a retail or entertainment website. Careful consideration might be made to ensure that the aesthetics or overall design of a site do not clash with the clarity and accuracy of the content or the ease of web navigation,. especially on a B2B website. Designers may also consider the reputation of the owner or business the site is representing to make sure they are portrayed favorably.

2. User experience design and interactive Design

User understanding of the content of a website often depends on user understanding of how the website works. This is part of the user experience design. User experience is related to layout, clear instructions and labeling on a website. How well a user understands how they can interact on a site may also depend on the interactive design of the site. If a user perceives the usefulness of the website, they are more likely to continue using it. Users who are skilled and well versed with website use may find a more distinctive, yet less intuitive or less user-friendly website interface useful nonetheless. However, users with less experience are less likely to see the advantages or usefulness of a less intuitive website interface. This drives the trend for a more universal user experience and ease of access to accommodate as many users as possible regardless of user skill.. Much of the user experience design and interactive design are considered in the user interface design.

Advanced interactive functions may require plug-ins if not advanced coding language skills. Choosing whether or not to use interactivity that requires plug-ins is a critical decision in user experience design. If the plug-in doesn't come pre-installed with most browsers, there's a risk that the user will have neither the know how or the patience to install a plug-in just to access the content. If the function requires advanced coding language skills, it may be too costly in either time or money to code compared to the amount of enhancement the function will add to the user experience. There's also a risk that advanced interactivity may be incompatible with older browsers or hardware configurations. Publishing a function that doesn't work reliably is potentially worse for the user experience than making no attempt. It depends on the target audience if it's likely to be needed or worth any risks.

3. Progressive enhancement

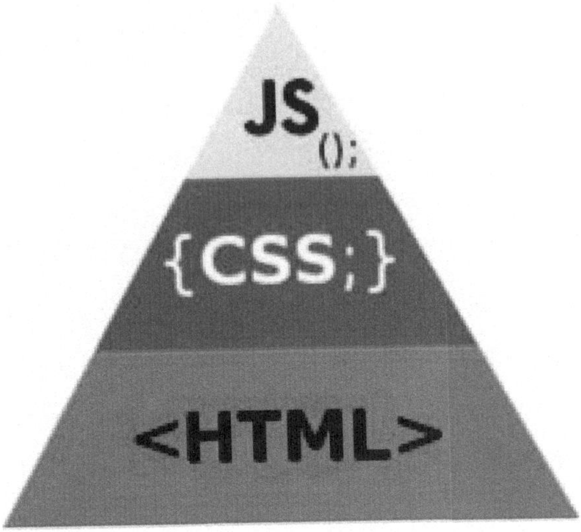

The order of progressive enhancement

Progressive enhancement is a strategy in web design that puts emphasis on web content first, allowing everyone to access the basic content and functionality of a web page, whilst users with additional browser features or faster Internet access receive the enhanced version instead.

In practice, this means serving content through HTML and applying styling and animation through CSS to the technically possible extent, then applying further enhancements through JavaScript. Pages' text is loaded immediately through the HTML source code rather than having to wait for JavaScript to initiate and load the content subsequently, which allows content to be readable with minimum loading time and bandwidth, and through text-based browsers, and maximizes backwards compatibility.

As an example, MediaWiki-based sites including Wikipedia use progressive enhancement, as they remain usable while JavaScript and even CSS is deactivated, as pages' content is included in the page's HTML source code, whereas counter-example Everipedia relies on JavaScript to load pages' content subsequently; a blank page appears with JavaScript deactivated.

Page layout

Part of the user interface design is affected by the quality of the page layout. For example, a designer may consider whether the site's page layout should remain consistent on different pages when designing the layout. Page pixel width may also be considered vital for aligning objects in the layout design. The most popular fixed-width websites generally have the same set width to match the current most popular browser window, at the current most popular screen resolution, on the current most popular monitor size. Most pages are also center-aligned for concerns of aesthetics on larger screens.

Fluid layouts increased in popularity around 2000 to allow the browser to make user-specific layout adjustments to fluid layouts based on the details of the reader's screen (window size, font size relative to window etc.). They grew as an alternative to HTML-table-based layouts and grid-based design in both page layout design principle and in coding technique, but were very slow to be adopted.. This was due to considerations of screen reading devices and varying windows sizes which designers have no control over. Accordingly, a design may be broken down into units (sidebars, content blocks, embedded advertising areas, navigation areas) that are sent to the browser and which will be fitted into the display window by the browser, as best it can. Although such a display may often change the relative position of major content units, sidebars may be displaced below body text rather than to the side of it. This is a more flexible display than a hard-coded grid-based layout that doesn't fit the device window. In particular, the relative position of content blocks may change while leaving the content within the block unaffected. This also minimizes the user's need to horizontally scroll the page.

Responsive web design is a newer approach, based on CSS3, and a deeper level of per-device specification within the page's style sheet through an enhanced use of the CSS @media rule. In March 2018 Google announced they would be rolling out mobile-first indexing.. Sites using responsive design are well placed to ensure they meet this new approach.

Typography

Web designers may choose to limit the variety of website typefaces to only a few which are of a similar style, instead of using a wide range of typefaces or type styles. Most browsers recognize a specific number of safe fonts, which designers mainly use in order to avoid complications.

Font downloading was later included in the CSS3 fonts module and has since been implemented in Safari 3.1, Opera 10 and Mozilla Firefox 3.5. This has subsequently increased interest in web typography, as well as the usage of font downloading. Most site layouts incorporate negative space to break the text up into paragraphs and also avoid center-aligned text.

Motion graphics

The page layout and user interface may also be affected by the use of motion graphics. The choice of whether or not to use motion graphics may depend on the target market for the website. Motion graphics may be expected or at least better received with an entertainment-oriented website. However, a website target audience with a more serious or formal interest (such as business, community, or government) might find animations unnecessary and distracting if only for entertainment or decoration purposes. This doesn't mean that more serious content couldn't be enhanced with animated or video presentations that is relevant to the content. In either case, motion graphic design may make the difference between more effective visuals or distracting visuals.

Motion graphics that are not initiated by the site visitor can produce accessibility issues. The World Wide Web consortium accessibility standards require that site visitors be able to disable the animations.

Quality of code

Website designers may consider it to be good practice to conform to standards. This is usually done via a description specifying what the element is doing. Failure to conform to standards may not make a website unusable or error prone, but standards can relate to the correct layout of pages for readability as well making sure coded elements are closed appropriately. This includes errors in code, more organized layout for code, and making sure IDs and classes are identified properly. Poorly coded pages are sometimes colloquially called tag soup. Validating via W3C. can only be done when a correct DOCTYPE declaration is made, which is used to highlight errors in code. The system identifies the errors and areas that do not conform to web design standards. This information can then be corrected by the user.

Generated content

There are two ways websites are generated:

- Static websites

A static website stores a unique file for every page of a static website. Each time that page is requested, the same content is returned. This content is created once, during the design of the website. It is usually manually authored, although some sites use an automated creation process, similar to a dynamic website, whose results are stored long-term as completed pages. These automatically created static sites became more popular around 2015, with generators such as Jekyll and Adobe Muse.

The benefits of a static website are that they were simpler to host, as their server only needed to serve static content, not execute server-side scripts. This required less server administration and had less chance of exposing security holes. They could also serve pages more quickly, on low-cost server hardware. These advantage became less important as cheap web hosting expanded to also offer dynamic features, and virtual servers offered high performance for short intervals at low cost.

Almost all websites have some static content, as supporting assets such as images and style sheets are usually static, even on a website with highly dynamic pages.

- **Dynamic websites**

Dynamic websites are generated on the fly and use server-side technology to generate webpages. They typically extract their content from one or more back-end databases: some are database queries across a relational database to query a catalogue or to summarise numeric information, others may use a document database such as MongoDB or NoSQL to store larger units of content, such as blog posts or wiki articles.

In the design process, dynamic pages are often mocked-up or wireframed using static pages. The skillset needed to develop dynamic web pages is much broader than for a static pages, involving server-side and database coding as well as client-side interface design. Even medium-sized dynamic projects are thus almost always a team effort.

When dynamic web pages first developed, they were typically coded directly in languages such as Perl, PHP or ASP. Some of these, notably PHP and ASP, used a 'template' approach where a server-side page resembled the structure of the completed client-side page and data was inserted into places defined by 'tags'. This was a quicker means of development than coding in a purely procedural coding language such as Perl.

Both of these approaches have now been supplanted for many websites by higher-level application-focused tools such as content management systems. These build on top of general purpose coding platforms and assume that a website exists to offer content according to one of several well recognised models, such as a time-sequenced blog, a thematic magazine or news site, a wiki or a user forum. These tools make the implementation of such a site very easy, and a purely organisational and design-based task, without requiring any coding.

Editing the content itself (as well as the template page) can be done both by means of the site itself, and with the use of third-party software. The ability to edit all pages is provided only to a specific category of users (for example, administrators, or registered users). In some cases, anonymous users are allowed to edit certain web content, which is less frequent (for example, on forums - adding messages). An example of a site with an anonymous change is Wikipedia.

Homepage design

Usability experts, including Jakob Nielsen and Kyle Soucy, have often emphasised homepage design for website success and asserted that the homepage is the most important page on a website..Nielsen, Jakob; Tahir, Marie (October 2001), Homepage Usability: 50 Websites Deconstructed, New Riders Publishing, ISBN 978-0735711020.. However practitioners into the 2000s were starting to find that a growing number of website traffic was bypassing the homepage, going directly to internal content pages through search engines, e-newsletters and RSS feeds.. Leading many practitioners to argue that homepages are less important than most people think..... Jared Spool argued in 2007 that a site's homepage was actually the least important page on a website.

In 2022 and 2023, carousels (also called 'sliders' and 'rotating banners') have become an extremely popular design element on homepages, often used to showcase featured or recent content in a confined space... Many practitioners argue that carousels are an ineffective design element and hurt a website's search engine optimisation and usability.

Occupations

There are two primary jobs involved in creating a website: the web designer job and web developer job, who often work closely together on a website. The web designers are responsible for the visual aspect, which includes the layout, coloring and the typography of a web page. Web designers will also have a working knowledge of markup languages such as HTML and CSS, although the extent of their knowledge will differ from one web designer to another. Particularly in smaller organizations, one person will need the necessary skills for designing and programming the full web page, while larger organizations may have a web designer responsible for the visual aspect alone.

Further jobs which may become involved in the creation of a website include:

- Graphic designers to create visuals for the site such as logos, layouts and buttons.

- Internet marketing specialists to help maintain web presence through strategic solutions on targeting viewers to the site, by using marketing and promotional techniques on the internet.

- SEO writers to research and recommend the correct words to be incorporated into a particular website and make the website more accessible and found on numerous search engines.

- Internet copywriter to create the written content of the page to appeal to the targeted viewers of the site.

- User experience (UX) designer incorporates aspects of user-focused design considerations which include information architecture, user-centered design, user testing, interaction design, and occasionally visual design.

Conversation with the Author

Karan: Hi, Ms. Sangeeta. How are you?

Sangeeta: I'm good. I'm good, Karan. How are you?

Karan: All good, all good.

Sangeeta: Great.

Karan: So, I've been following you on Instagram and Facebook. I came across you and I'm really glad to know about the work that you know, the work you just did and you are working on currently, based on that, actually, I'm writing a book, so I would like to take your interview and, you know, kind of an influence, influence, I want some workings, insights of you for the work basically.

Speaker 1: How lovely!

Speaker 2: So, if you are good can I ask you some questions?

Sangeeta: Sure, I'm happy to, you know, answer all your questions. I'm happy to be here.

Speaker 2: Thank you. Thank you so much. So what business are you into basically?

Sangeeta: Actually, I'm into digital marketing and social media marketing line of Business.

Speaker 2: OK. OK, nice. How long have you have been into this business...? How did you get into this business?

Sangeeta: Actually, it has been nine years my brother Ajay Tejwani, started in USA in San Antonio, Texas and you know in year 2011, print was dying its own death. I am a marketing professional and have a huge experience in Marketing and brand positioning. At the time I was in print media, at the time the top most newspaper - I was working as an Account Group Manager in Gulf News and then I worked in the Concierge-four languages, and Dubai Mall magazine. I was initially working with the main newspaper - with Aquarius Magazine and later with the magazines catering to tourists which were then 20 million compared to residents only 4 million population, and I was handling Dubai Mall magazine and to Concierge magazine. The print has been the medium to communicate and promote at the that time and then like everything has a start and end, print was eroding from the market. The impact was slowly eroding as it is one way communication from the journalist to their Target audience. However, digital/Social media, which makes everyone a journalist - a voice to speak to the world, everyone is empowered-that really intrigued me. I wanted to contribute to the businesses by delivering ROI to every company/ business owner with numbers which were not available with print at all.

I think they are the most beautiful human race alive and got lost due to the hype of Hollywood. For the media agencies- the margins are high in print, billboards, moppies etc., but Digital the margins are non- existing as it is all transparent. I got into digital and online media and luckily my brother offered me handholding in the beginning. A medium which talks numbers and that's how I got into it, and we are now a nine-year-old company day in and day out we breathe ROI. We were lucky to work with bignames like World Trade Centre, Microsoft and many more that too initially in our business starting point. Also, we were part of and launched many start-ups and E-commerce companies in UAE. We are in have a full-fledged office in JLT, we have in-House team of 17 professionals. Our goal is to deliver Success every time and every day! And yeah, we really are happy with the progress and the number of years of experience which we have in converting clients ROI'S and sales.

At Digital Media Sapiens, from last 9 years we have been generating qualified leads, we have been working with Gulf Food at World Trade Center, Gitex and other events. We have been selected as a Microsoft preferred partner agency for their 33 Gold partners. We have worked with some big names and startups as well as we believe all that is small or start up will grow and become big with right ROI delivered for their brands. We breathe ROI, we think ROI, we are a ROI driven company.

Our team works together, fights together, Enjoys together, has fun together and celebrate the success for client's every time they send us a cool email or a surprise cake to unlimited pampering with food and drinks all day at Kempinski hotel at MOE etc. Client success is what we enjoy the most. Contact us for more.

Our thermometer of our business success is our clients doubling their profits.

Speaker 1: What to check while selecting a digital marketing agency?

Sangeeta: Question many of our clients ask us as to - How to select a high performing digital marketing agency?

The first thing you have to know is as to how many years of experience the agency has.

Secondly, the profile and collective experience of their team. The team is more important and of course, if the C.E.O and the management is ambitious, their credentials, certifications and experience are.

Third thing is, if they have credibility of working with government, semi-government, local experience, international brands etc. And years of experience of working in your vertical or with your competitors.

Fourth thing is of course, their clients. What kind of clients do they have? And you know, if at all, you can talk to their clients and get their feedback.

Are they systems oriented or people oriented? What is their reporting and progression system?

And in a digital agency mostly, you have to navigate to get things done.

Speaker 1: What are Google ads?

Sangeeta: Google ads are search ads, display ads, shopping ads, these are the basic 3 types of ads.
Search ads are the search, when you are searching on the google, you know, search engine, the search ads appear and then the shopping ads are images of, it's mainly for the E-Commerce, all the images which are appearing and display ads are when you are reading an article and you see a display ad following you.

So, yeah! We can use display ads and search ads for remarketing as well on google. So, google is the great engine which gets you qualified leads because people are searching for your services and they are on google searching for your service and if they are not closing with you, they are closing with your competition. So, it's a very good idea to be on top of

your brand keywords and your competitor keywords on the search engines.
To know more, contact us.

Speaker 2: Nice and so how do you enjoy your job? What do you enjoy about your job basically?

Sangeeta: I really enjoy digital marketing because I love numbers, I love sales, I am standing for the success of all our clients. Sometimes, due to their lack of vision and focus, mainly the growth plan, we are not able to make the difference, which I want to. That is the only challenge we are facing right now.

I used to work in Gulf news but now I am happy that I am able to contribute to so many businesses and increase their sales and that's what I stand for, that's what I live for, that's what gives me happiness to make you successful and also happy.

What I enjoy right now is learning every day one new thing and speed of implementation of it. And the day I am not learning, that day is the death.

Speaker 1: (laughter) Ok, I would not suggest you direct this. Keep on learning more and more. And what are the most exciting advances in your industry right now?

Sangeeta: Most exciting is artificial intelligence with chatbots and WhatsApp which has really made a 4X difference in our clients ROI. The other thing which is fabulous is metaverse which is like avatars which I want to talk a little more in the conversation.

Speaker 1: What is an AI bot?

An AI bot can really increase minimum atleast 4x of your business. It responds instead of a human being on your behalf and it keeps learning the answers which humans are giving to the questions asked and due to its constant learning capabilities it keeps adapting and learning. And then if the same question is pooping up again, the bot will answer the same like a human would answer. No human interaction at this time, so, your cost goes down gradually and your sales go up. And I really, highly recommend it. It is a software that interacts with human, through written language. It is often imbedded in web pages. The digital application of answers to the customer inquiries without the use of, without the need of human agents and providing affordable customer service on time, every time, 24x7.

So, you know, it's a conversation that includes E-Commerce sites, and bots allow customers to ask questions about a particular product and give the answers at the same moment which could be night or day, anywhere in the work round the clock. I am sure this is just the beginning.

Speaker 2: Make sure, and what changes have you seen over the last few years?

Sangeeta: In our industry, there is a change every hour, every minute and, you know, there are lots of changes happening all the time. So, your right answer yesterday is the wrong answer today!

AI is a massively scaled and interoperable network of real-time rendered 3D virtual worlds that can be experienced precisely at the same time and persistently by an effectively unlimited number of users with an individual sense of presence and with continuity of data, such as identity, history, entitlements, objects, communications, and payments.

Either way, you look at it, the metaverse is going to change our world, with VR headsets, or AR glasses.

Meta remains confident that it will be a thing of the present and not the future. We'll see VR that will draw people into the experience.

And as I said, it's more of a metaverse. So we'll be having avatars of ourselves – an avatar who can perform, feel and experience everything just like we do. And with a blink of an eye, with our meta contact lenses, we'll be in the Internet world and we can experience it emotionally, mentally, physically, and experience all of it, you know, wherever we want to travel, attend an event etc. So we can attend an event in Sydney, we can attend a meeting in New York or Los Angeles by just sitting in our House. We can also experience and feel in Bali at the beach the cool breeze - you know, the beach just being in our house.

Speaker 2: Oh nice. That's great.

Speaker 1: Yeah.

Karan: Without leaving would you want to experience things staying in home?

Sangeeta: I mean, you can. If you want to – so you have now a choice. If you don't have time and you want to, there is a choice- what I'm saying and if you want to go, of course you can, or you know both ways. So yeah, metaverse is a new reality. An avatar created of your identity, feels and knows exactly what you know so life can mean 2X you.

Karan: OK. Well, that's nice. And what challenges have you overcome in the last few years?

Sangeeta: So everything which goes up comes down. You know, the whole pre-COVID and COVID situation was huge because we had lots of event companies and you know, and then we are you know... in the journey of improvement, so the whole company went through a lot of improvement. We have totally automated our systems which has helped us a lot in getting closer to client happiness because our clients are very ambitious. They're happy with the numbers which they are getting today, but they want to go very big. So, to manage that, you know we have to all the time grow ourselves and close the gap between client expectations and our performance. So yeah, if you are passionate and are ahead of change-you can win the game.

Karan: And based on your experience, where do you think your industry will go next?

Sangeeta: As I said, you know you can attend everything you know being at home and you know you can just go to a transformational metaverse. So the Internet never actually ceases to amaze me and you can experience the Internet power in the virtual world and the separation between them is getting completely closed. So the reality and the real reel are one thing.

Karan: Yes.

Sangeeta: You will be having an avatar, and your avatar will be you like. Sangeeta will be totally feeling like what I'm feeling. My avatar will be feeling my emotions, my feelings, my experiences and you know I can experience the whole world just by being me.

Be Uniquely You! Your avatar is a digital expression of your personality (or personalities). It can convey how much of an extrovert or introvert you are, your sense of humor, and even your fashion sense. It lets you be your authentic self, and that in turn can help you connect more meaningfully with your friends, family, coworkers, or anyone else you meet on the road to the metaverse.

We want to enable everyone to present the best version of themselves, which is why we've made it possible to customize your avatar with a wide variety of free outfits and accessories. Feel like giving yourself blue hair today, trying out new makeup or sporting a suit for a professional look? No problem — you can customize your avatar anytime you want to suit your mood. In fact, with more than a quintillion combinations of free avatar options already available, your choices will almost certainly be uniquely yours.

We also know that people often want to change their look, whether in the real world or in digital spaces. One way we'll make that evolution easier is by continually offering new options that reflect the latest sartorial trends and expanding to offer more outfits from fashion, hairstyle, sports and lifestyle brands, etc. over time.

The new Meta Avatars will roll out in the coming weeks on Instagram, Facebook, and Messenger. Learn how to create avatar for Instagram, Facebook and Messenger. And we expect Meta to bring it to VR soon. So keep an eye out for it when it becomes available for you.

Speaker 2: Yes, I Would definitely like to have a sense of that. How does that work

Sangeeta: Of course.

Speaker 2: What are some of the best experiences you have had with your clients and your business?

Sangeeta: The best experiences? Uh, you're in which question?

Speaker 2: 7.

Sangeeta: OK. So the best experiences are basically the ROI and the sales which we have achieved and like with clients like World Trade Center, Microsoft Office their Gold Partners, Lookswoow, etc., some of them I can't name due to NDA signed with them. So they have grown huge from where they were to where they are in terms of numbers ROI, we are a numbers company. So the ROI they have achieved is like 700%.

Speaker 2: Oh wow! That's huge.

Sangeeta: Yeah.

Speaker 1: And what are some of the results that your clients benefit....client's business have had?

Sangeeta: So they actually started multiple locations, multiple offices and huge growth and they're still growing.

Speaker 2: Well, that's great.This is one of the biggest motive actually, for a business is that your client's grow much more. That gives me happiness-My team and I added value to their business.

Sangeeta: True. That's true.

Speaker 1: So, uh, how do? I think it's like how have your clients been changed by your products service that you offer?

Sangeeta: The client has changed basically, you know, what we offer is, you know, changing their whole business model and we also do a consultation with the clients so that, you know, they can, they can not only get the sales but they are also able to convert the sales. So we actually, which is not even part of our scope, but we actually do training for their sales team and their tele-sales team so they can convert more. Sales is just numbers if you can improve the percentage of conversion by 5% or 10% you are already on 4X bottom line profits. And also we tell them the loopholes that they can improve in their business which is basically on their websites, you know anywhere from lead to final sale, sometimes holistic approach helps, the communication in their online and offline presence, in their story, their creatives, everything how they present themselves. So holistic Omni channel targeting is what we do. So that they can thrive and as a brand and as a they can get more of their market share compared to their competitors and we also keep them ahead of the game by implementing new things because our head office is in the USA. So we know what's happening on Facebook and Instagram in the beta stage and we keep our clients ahead of their competitors all the time.

Speaker 2: Well, that's it. That helps them a lot, it’s a whole new dimension

Sangeeta: True.

Speaker 1: What is the difference between organic traffic and paid traffic?

Sangeeta: You know, S.E.O is organic traffic which depends on the trust value the brand has in the internet and among people. While paid traffic is S.E.M which includes Facebook ads, Instagram ads, Tik-Tok ads, snap chat ads and google ads it also includes, story ads, remarketing, retargeting. Additionally, we use lot of paid tools to know the movements blue prints of your clients to their mouse navigations on your website with videos recording of their mouse tracking the navigation and eye prints of your clients on your website. Which is then used to target them as per NeuroScience and psychology of buying behaviour of each client is different then others like what time they are in learning mode, knowing more mode, browsing mode and actually buying mode to the level what time they normally are actively searching for your goods or services and what time they are binge watching on Netflix and are not going to respond to your ads. The buckets of all this data are created for their online footprints which includes google maps and knowing their persona to what they like and don't. And this data we can use to target them accordingly.

Speaker 2: And what are some of the learnings and strategies that have radically impacted your business?

Sangeeta: There are three things. One is, you know, business automation, which has really helped us a lot to make everything easy, you know, systematic with the checklist (daily, weekly and monthly) and with the Flowchart management system and Project Management System you know our team get scores whether they are in green, yellow or red. Team also wants to perform. The problem is we don't know how to communicate and make them perform and get the best out of them. And in our agency we follow the client first approach, client FIRST. And beyond the client, as the client as a person, so their business FIRST approach is pivotal. So we consult the client for the business growth, sometimes not even limiting to them as a person, but you know focused on transformation and getting attached to the results for their business. So yeah, this is approach and team mindset has really helped them and helped us and this is also transformed their business and most important thing also is very important is happy team, so happy team behind the clients growth, do a turbo charging the clients growth. So, we cannot work alone, we have to work together to achieve the results.

Speaker 2: That's great. That's also, That's a great strategy also.

Sangeeta: Yeah. the only pleasure is client success and their growth.

Speaker 2: So if you have to start all over again, what would you do differently?

Sangeeta: Yes, I would have implemented all the systems first, which we did not at that time- so we were people's company rather than systems. Ensuring that implement all the systems, invest in the systems you know, as this the backbone of any company and think it's an investment and not a cost. Second thing is you know, I would recommend having an investor, so that I can in the first go, so that I can have multiple offices and multiply them, so we can help as many clients as we can, through that expansion in different markets. Yeah, and I would also have... I mean, I would also probably have, be in front of camera, podcasts and written books on digital marketing before I actually started the company so that I can help people who can't even you know who can't. I can. I cannot help them with digital marketing.

So I can help them with my book and my videos, podcasts, you know? And being consistent with it.. So every year there is a new launch, new challenge, new growth, new learning. So I would love to share that with all my friends,as many people/companies as I can help.

Speaker 2: That's great. That's awesome and what would be your advice to people who are starting a new business in your industry?

Sangeeta: The first thing is client feedback forms. You should have the client feedback forms and the client will guide you where you are lacking what you're lacking and the client's first approach. And always make sure that your team is learning something new every day with weekly innovation day.

Speaker 2: Great, great. Those were great insights Sangeeta ji! And it was an honor to actually take an interview. I would definitely include lots and lots of points of yours in my upcoming journal. And I would also like it if you could help me with some of your friends or some of the other industry leaders, who are in your circle or who can help me with this journal.

Sangeeta: Sure, sure, sure, sure. Thank you so much for your time, Karan, and it's a pleasure being with you. Thank you.

Karan 2: Thank you. Thank you so much.

Author Bio

Meet Sangeeta Butani, a digital marketing expert with over 13 years of experience in the industry. With a keen eye for detail and a passion for creativity, Sangeeta Butani has been helping businesses of all sizes to achieve their digital marketing goals and drive growth through strategic campaigns.

With a deep understanding of the latest trends and best practices, Sangeeta has helped countless clients to stay ahead of the curve and outperform their competitors.

But it's not just about the work for Sangeeta Butani. In addition to being a digital marketing professional, Sangeeta is also an avid traveler and have traveled to 62 countries, foodie, and lover of all things tech. When Sangeeta is not busy crafting killer marketing campaigns, you can find her exploring new destinations or trying out the latest gadgets.

With a proven track record of success, a passion for innovation, and a personality that shines both online and off, Sangeeta is the ideal partner to take digital marketing to the next level and can help you achieve your goals and grow your business.

Sangeeta Butani is an expert in Generating Sales Leads, Clients and Revenue using Omnichannel Digital Strategies. Passionate Digital Marketer- Serial Entrepreneur. Thrive on TURBO charging Digital ROI for all our clients. whose accomplishments include:

Education:

- Degree in Business Management and Economics from Jesus and Mary College (Delhi)

- Massachusetts Institute of Technology
  PGDD, Digital Transformation 2013 - 2014
  Grade: 92% Grade A Grade: 92% Grade A

- National Institute of Information Technology
  Diploma in Software coding and programming,
  Coding in Cobol and Java script

Work History:

- 26+ years of experience in various verticals at multiple positions
- Google Preferred Partner Agency 2013

Awards, Titles, and Designations:

- Google Analytic Certified
- Bexar county GOLD AWARD
- Best Social Media Agency EXCELLENCE AWARD by Global foods industries Issued Jan 2018

Personal Info:

Passionate Digital Marketer, having 9+ years of experience in Digital Marketing. Prior to this, she has worked in GULF NEWS, Dubai Mall magazine. Specialized in leadership, highly motivated professional.

- Worked with corporations, including Gulf News-Al Nisr Publishing, Nicholas Publishing and American Express etc.
- Her first business which is running now with offices in San Antonio, Texas and an office in Dubai from the past 12 years. Had a huge growth in the first 6 years and before 2019 had a downfall due to events and malls being closed.
- Read over 68+ books in a span of 1-2 years when things were not going as expected in the business which altered the perception about business completely and that's where the turnaround started.
- Have helped and worked with over 350+ businesses and helped them grow their profits anywhere from 17% to over 200%

To be successful at **Lead Generation using Google, Social, Programmatic, Affiliate. Omnichannel Marketing channels, Online Media Buying,** all you need is instruction and encouragement from someone who has "been there and done that!".

And as you can see from above, **Omnichannel Digital Marketing professional - Sangeeta Butani** is uniquely qualified to help you understand everything you need to know about The PROVEN System to Generate high value Sales Leads, Clients and Revenue using all online platforms!

9 789362 611420

Printed at Repro India Ltd.